KONDITORI

Pastry Shop

By
Catherine W.

Published by:

Catherine W.
Po Box 44692
Boise, ID 83711

© 2009 All Rights Reserved.
ISBN: 978-0-578-01315-2

Cover C.W.

Website: www.cwkitchen.net

Printed in United States of America

Thank you...

...to all my friends and customers
that supported me while Konditori was open.

To Marika & Kris Gethin:
Thank you for all the encouragement, and for the amazing
friendship we have established.

To Brandi Wilson:
Thank you for the great friendship we created in such a short time.
Thank you for all the good laughs we shared, I truly missed them everyday!

To Birgitta Clark:
It has been my pleasure to bring you a
piece of good memories from home to your heart again.

NOTES

I love to spend time in my kitchen,

because in my kitchen I create magic with my hands, and pour my love into what I do.

I later fill my friends with the love that was created by my hands. Who doesn't love a wedge of freshly baked goods, everybody does.

Konditori is now making it available for you to make the *Old World Style* baked goods with a few shortcuts in your own kitchen.

When something seem to be too complicated it surprises you how truly easy it can be.

Why settle for less when you can make the best.

Everyone talks about techniques, when it really is all about following directions, nothing is impossible; all you need is the time and a smidge of patience.

The book is focusing on giving you the tools to make it yourself. It will have *Konditori's* secret recipes, equipment list that is essential for a baker, shortcuts, and list of where to find special ingredients.

Notes to You...

The importance of measuring products is essential in baking. If you are asked to use ounces, fl ounces, then scale and use the correct measure. Not all products works well by measuring cups, because many times we tend to pack flours too hard and you end up having more flour in the recipe than you really should have had. Don't guess the estimation because too much of something ruins the intended texture of the final product.

In my recipes I use mostly butter with salt, if I use unsalted butter it will say that, so don't use unsalted butter unless it is specifically stated. Eggs; I always use large eggs, unless it is stated something different.

A few things I would have as for starter tools in my kitchen is for a baker: A mixer, one rolling pin with handles, a scale, a set of measuring spoons, and 1 quart measuring cup for fluids.

NOTES

Sweet Breads

Sweet Rolls

Cardamom Braid w/ Almond Paste

2 tbsp dry instant SAF™ yeast
2 cups milk
5 oz butter
4 oz sugar
1 tsp salt
2.8 lbs all purpose flour
3 eggs
1 tbsp cardamom

Filling:
10.2 oz butter

Yield: 8

4 tbsp cinnamon
3 oz granulated sugar
4 oz almond paste
2 tbsp cardamom

Topping:
3 oz pearl sugar
2 oz sliced almonds
1 egg
1 tsp water

Oven temperature:
Gas or Electric Oven: 425° F,
Second Lowest Rack, Bake
time 15-18 minutes

Directions:

Put the yeast in the mixing bowl add sugar. Melt the butter, pour the milk over it.

Pour the milk mixture over the yeast and sugar, add the eggs. Whisk in the eggs with the other wet ingredients.

Mix the flour with salt and cardamom. Pour it into the wet ingredients. Attach the dough hook, and let it knead for 10 minutes.

When done kneading, remove the dough hook. Pull out the dough onto the counter, and kneed it together into a big smooth ball.

Let it proof for 45 minutes. Divided the dough in half, and roll it out with a rolling pin, size approx. 40 inches by 8 inches.

Make the filling:

Mix the butter and the cinnamon. Use half of the mix, and spread it evenly over the dough.

Sprinkle 1 tbsp cardamom onto the dough, and 1 ½ oz of granulated sugar.

Take 2 oz of almond paste and layer it on the edge of the dough closest to you, roll the dough up into a long cylinder shaped log.

Take your scissor, and start snipping the dough with the scissor.

Make the snip half way into the dough, then move the slice to the left side, and snip another piece the same way, and move that slice to the right side, do so over and over again, until you have done so with the entire log.

Cut the long braid into 4 pieces approx 10 inches long per braid.

Place 3 braids onto a parchment paper lined half sheet pan. Let the braids rest for 20 minutes.

Repeat the same procedure with the other half of the dough. Preheat the oven.

Mix the egg and the water for the egg wash, and brush the braids, sprinkle pearl sugar and sliced almonds. Bake the braids on the second lowest shelf for 15-18 minutes or until they are golden brown.

Sister Cake w/ Raisins & Bavarian Cream

2 tbsp dry instant SAF™ yeast
10.2 oz butter
4 tbsp cinnamon
1 cup raisins
3 oz granulated sugar
2 tbsp cardamom

Filling:
10.2 oz butter
4 tbsp cinnamon
1 cup raisins
3 oz granulated sugar
2 tbsp cardamom

Yield: 4-5 cakes

Oven temperature:
Gas or Electric Oven: 400° F,
Second Lowest Rack, Bake
time 20-25 min

Directions:

Put the yeast in the mixing bowl add sugar.

Melt the butter, pour the milk over it.

Pour the milk mixture over the yeast and sugar, add the eggs. Whisk in the eggs with the other wet ingredients.

Mix the flour with salt and cardamom. Pour it into the wet ingredients.

Attach the dough hook, and let it knead for 10 minutes.

When done kneading, remove the dough hook. Pull out the dough onto the counter, and kneed it together into a big smooth ball.

Let it proof for 45 minutes. Divided the dough in half, and roll it out with a rolling pin, size approx. 25 inches by 12 inches.

Topping:
1 egg
1 tsp water
1 small box of Vanilla Jell-O™
1 cup whole milk
1 cup of powdered sugar
2.5 tbsp water

Great tip is to use disposable cake pans from the grocery stores. Since you are lining them with parchment paper you can reuse them.

Make the filling:

Mix the butter and the cinnamon. Use half of the mix, and spread it evenly over the dough.

Sprinkle 1 tbsp of cardamom onto the dough, and 1 ½ oz of granulated sugar. Take ½ cup of raisins and sprinkle them evenly over the entire dough.

Roll the dough up into a long cylinder shaped log. Cut 1 inch thick pieces and place 8 pieces with the sliced side up and together in a round paper mold or place them in a parchment

paper lined cake pan with 1 ½ inch high wall. Repeat the same procedure with rest of the other dough.

Mix together a small package 3.4 oz of vanilla Jell-O™ with 1 cup of whole milk.

Use a 1 ½ tablespoon size ice cream scoop, and lay on scoop of the vanilla Jell-O™ cream mixture on each round bun.

Preheat the oven. Mix the egg and the water for the egg wash, and brush the cakes. Bake the cakes on the second lowest shelf for 15-25 minutes or until they are golden brown.

Mix together the powdered sugar and water. When the cakes have cooled down then drizzle the sugar glaze on top of the cakes.

Twisted Cinnamon Rolls

2 tbsp dry instant SAF™ yeast
2 cups milk
5 oz butter
4 oz sugar
1 tsp salt
2.1 lbs all purpose flour
1 egg
1 tbsp cardamom

Yield: 40 Rolls

Oven temperature:
Gas or Electric Oven:
450° F; Second Lowest
Rack,

Directions:

Put the yeast in the mixing bowl add sugar.

Melt the butter, pour the milk over it.

Pour the milk mixture over the yeast and sugar, add the eggs. Whisk in the eggs with the other wet ingredients.

Mix the flour with salt and cardamom. Pour it into the wet ingredients.

Attach the dough hook, and let it knead for 10 minutes.

When done kneading, remove the dough hook. Pull out the dough onto the counter, and kneed it together into a big smooth ball.

Let it proof for 45 minutes. Divided the dough in half, and roll it out with a rolling pin, size approx. 20 inches by 15 inches.

Filling:
10.2 oz butter
4 tbsp cinnamon
3 oz granulated sugar
2 tbsp cardamom

Topping:
3 oz pearl sugar
2 eggs
1 ½ tsp water

Make the filling:

Mix the butter and the cinnamon. Use half of the mix, and spread it evenly over the dough.

Sprinkle 1 tbsp of cardamom onto the dough, and 1 ½ oz of granulated sugar.

Fold half of the dough sheet over, the two sides with spread are now pressed onto each other. You should now have a flat sheet in the size of 20 inches by 7.5 inches.

Use your pastry cutter and slice 1 inch by 7.5 inch slices of the dough strips
(you should have about 20 slices).
Take the dough strip and twist it a few times, then hold one side of the dough strip and twist the twisted strip around your index finger and your middle finger until you run out of dough. Place each roll on parchment paper lined sheet pans.

Repeat the same procedure with the remainder of the strips, and do the same with the other part of the dough. Preheat the oven.

Mix the egg and the water for the egg wash, and brush the rolls, and sprinkle pearl sugar on top. Bake the rolls in the middle of the oven for 8-10 minutes.

Danishes

(Danish: Wienerbrød)
(Swedish: Wienerbröd)

1 cup whole milk
1.75 oz of fresh yeast
(wet yeast)
2 tbsp or granulated sugar
1 egg
10 oz margarine or butter

1 lb all purpose white flour
1 tsp cardamom
1 oz of all purpose flour
to mix in with the butter

Filling:
Raspberry or Apple Filling

Topping:
1 cup of powdered sugar
½ - 1 tbsp water

> OBS! Dry yeast does
> not work in this recipe.

Yield: 16 Large Danishes

The margarine or butter is mixed with 1oz of flour, and then spread it out on a wax paper, shaped as a square, about ½ - inch thick. Wrap up the margarine and let it firm up again.

For the dough:
 ALL ingredients should be well chilled. Dissolve the fresh yeast in the cold milk.
Add the egg and the sugar into the milk mixture.

Place all the flour in a large bowl add the cardamom, use a balloon whisk to fluff the flour, this way you don't need to sift the flour.
 Make a well in the flour; pour the milk mixture into the flour. The dough should be mixed together quickly and leave a nice shine to it, do not kneed it, this dough is not like other bread dough's.

Roll out the dough into a large square, 5/8 inch thick.

 Place the square butter so it covers half of the yeast dough. Fold over the other half.
The dough is now rolled out in an even and smooth motion to a large surface, approx. 1/3 inches thick and make a three fold. Cover the dough, before placing it in the refrigerator.

 After each fold you let the dough rest for 10-15 minutes in the refrigerator.
When rolling out the dough. Dust the table before placing the dough on the table. However, be careful to not use too much flour.

 Roll out the dough the last time into a large square, 16 inches by 16 inches.
Cut the dough into 4 x 4 squares and fold the corners into the middle.
Place a dollop of apple or raspberry filling.

 Preheat the oven. While the oven is preheating the Danishes gets a moment to rise about 10 minutes.
Egg wash the Danishes, and bake them in the middle of the oven.

Simple Danishes

3.52 oz butter
11.65 oz all purpose flour
2 tbsp granulated Sugar
1.76 oz fresh yeast (wet yeast)
2.53 fl oz milk cream (50% milk & 50% cream)
2 eggs

Filling:
3.52 oz butter
1 cup powdered sugar
2 tsp cardamom
1 tsp vanilla sugar

Egg wash:
1 egg
½ tsp water

Oven temperature:
Gas or Electric Oven: 450° F
Second Lowest Rack, 8 minutes

OBS! Dry yeast does
not work in this recipe.

Work in the butter into the flour. Add the sugar.
Dissolve the yeast into the cold milk.
Add the milk and the eggs to the flour mixture. Mix all ingredients together quickly to a smooth dough.

Roll out the dough to 12 x 16 inch rectangle shaped sheet.
Mix together butter, powdered sugar, cardamom, and vanilla. Spread the mixture over the sheet.
Roll it up, and cut the cylinder in to approx 20 pieces.
Place the pieces with the cut edge upwards in the paper baking molds.
Let them rest and rise for 1 hour in room temperature.

Turn on the oven to 450° F when there is 30 minutes left for the Danishes to rise.

Mix together ½ tsp water with 1 egg for the egg wash.

Before putting the Danishes in the oven egg wash them on top.

Bake them in the oven for 8 minutes.

Tip: You can make the same glaze for these Danishes as you have for the authentic Danishes on page 13, to drizzle on top.

Saffron Cats

2 tbsp dry instant SAF™ yeast
3.52 oz butter
2 cups milk
8.8 oz low fat quark
1 tsp Saffron
½ cup granulated sugar
½ tsp salt
2.1 lb all purpose flour
Raisins

Topping:
1 egg
½ tsp water

Oven temperature:
Gas or Electric Oven: 425 °F
Second Lowest Rack, 7 minutes

Put the yeast in the mixing bowl add sugar.

Melt the butter, pour the milk over it.

Pour the milk mixture over the yeast and sugar, saffron. Whisk in the quark with the other wet ingredients.

Add all the flour and the salt.

Attach the dough hook, and let it knead for 10 minutes.

When done kneading, remove the dough hook. Pull out the dough onto the counter, and kneed it together into a big smooth ball.

Let it proof for 40 minutes. Divided the dough in to 20 pieces. Roll out each piece to a long worm shape. Roll in one side of the ends towards the middle, like a wheel. Roll the other side the same way but on the opposite side of the other roll wheel.

Place a raisin in middle of each 'wheel'. Let them rest and rise for 20 – 30 minutes.

Turn on the oven to 425 °F degrees while they are rising.

Mix together ½ tsp water with 1 egg for the egg wash.

Brush your saffron cats with the egg wash and bake them in the oven for 7 minutes.

English Scones

14.55 oz flour
1/3 cup granulated sugar
½ tsp salt
2 ½ tsp baking powder
½ tsp baking soda
6 oz butter
¼ cup fresh squeeze orange juice and zest of the 1 orange
¾ cup low fat buttermilk
½ cup cranberries

Glaze:
½ cup of powdered sugar
½ tbsp water

Turn on the oven to 400 °F

Mix the flour, sugar, salt, baking powder, baking soda
Cut up the butter, add that to the dry mix, and let the mixer incorporate the butter into the flour.
Zest the orange; add the zest to the flour mix.
Add the dry cranberries into the mix.
Mix the orange juice with the butter milk.
Add the buttermilk to the flour mix; let the mixer incorporate it all.

Roll out the dough to a disc 1 inch thick and stamp out rounds with a biscuit cutter, depending on the size of the cutter regulates the amount of how many you can get out of this dough.

If you do it by weight you can get 17, 2 oz scones. This dough is approx. 34 oz.

Place the scones on a parchment paper line baking sheet; place no more than 12 on a sheet.

Bake them in the oven for 15-17 minutes depending on size.

Glaze the scones as soon as they get out of the oven with a brush. Let them cool off completely before eating. The scones are "carry over cooking" on the baking sheet so they don't get too dry. The scones are supposed to be lighter and airier.

> **STOP:** *You can make many varieties Cranberry Orange, Blueberry Orange, Blueberry Lemon, Apple Strawberries, Apricot Pineapple, and Cherry Vanilla.*
> *When it comes to the juices replace the orange juice with lemon juice or apple juice or apple cider, vanilla, or pineapple juice.*
> *You can also replace the orange zest with lemon zest if you use the lemon juice*

Pumpkin Spice Scones

14.55 oz flour
1/3 cup granulated sugar
½ tsp salt
2 ½ tsp baking powder
½ tsp baking soda
1 tsp ground pumpkin spice
½ tsp ground cinnamon
6 oz butter
1/8 cup fresh squeeze orange juice
¾ cup low fat buttermilk
1/3 cup pumpkin puree

Glaze:
1 cup of powdered sugar
2 tbsp molasses
1 tbsp of maple syrup
1 ½ tsp water

Turn on the oven to 400 °F

Mix the flour, sugar, salt, baking powder, baking soda, spices
Cut up the butter, add that to the dry mix, and let the mixer incorporate the butter into the flour.
Mix the orange juice with the butter milk, and the pumpkin puree.
Add the buttermilk mix to the flour mix; let the mixer incorporate it all.

Roll out the dough to a disc 1 inch thick and stamp out rounds with a biscuit cutter, depending on the size of the cutter regulates the amount of how many you can get out of this dough.

If you do it by weight you can get 10, 3 oz scones. This dough is approx. 30 oz.

Place the scones on a parchment paper line baking sheet; place no more than 12 on a sheet.

Bake them in the oven for 17-19 minutes depending on size.

While the scones are baking make the glaze by mixing all the ingredients together.
The glaze should be thicker, and drizzled in a pattern over the scones.
The scones need to cool off a little before adding the glaze.

NOTES

Breads

Walnut Cranberry Bread

Oven temperature:
Gas or Electric Oven: 425° F
Second Lowest Rack 20-25 minutes

2 tbsp dry instant SAF™ yeast
20.3 fl oz (600 ml) warm water
2 tsp granulated sugar
½ tbsp salt
1 lb 9 oz white bread flour
6 tbsp cranberries
1 cup of coarsely chopped walnuts

Egg wash:
1 egg
½ tsp water

Put the dry instant yeast in the mixing bowl and add the sugar.

Pour the water mixture over the yeast and sugar. Whisk together the wet ingredients.

Mix 1 lb and 3 oz of flour with the salt, add that to the wet ingredients.

Attach the dough hook, and let it knead for 10 minutes.

Last 2 minutes add the walnuts and the cranberries.

When done kneading, remove the dough hook. Pull out the dough onto the counter, and kneed it together into a big smooth ball. Let is rest and rise for 45 minutes.

Divide the dough into two equal parts. Kneed it together in to two rounds.

Place the rounds on a parchment paper lined baking sheet, let them rise for 15 – 20 minutes uncovered.

Turn on the oven to 425° F.

Mix the egg and water for the egg wash. Brush the bread with the egg wash.

Bake the bread in the oven, second lowest rack, for 20 – 25 minutes.

Let the bread rest on the sheet pan for 5 minutes then move them to a wire rack and let them finish cooling off.

Carrot Bread w/ Thyme

2 tbsp dry instant SAF™ yeast
2 oz butter
1 cup water
1 cup milk
2 tbsp Lyles Golden Syrup
1 tbsp salt
1 tbsp thyme, dry
1¼ cups carrots, shredded
2 cups whole wheat flour
3 cups unbleached bread flour

Egg wash and topping:
1 egg
½ tsp sea salt & thyme

<u>Oven temperature:</u>
<u>For 3 breads</u>
Gas or Electric Oven: 425° F
Second Lowest Rack 17-19 minutes
<u>For Buns</u>
Gas or Electric Oven: 450° F
Second Lowest Rack 12 minutes

Melt the butter, add the milk and water. The temperature should be warm, but not hot.
Place the yeast in the mixing bowl; pour the liquid over the yeast.
Add now the syrup, stir it in.
Mix the salt with the wheat flour, carrots, and thyme. Add 3 cups of the regular flour.
Mix it all up.

Add all the dry ingredients to the wet ingredients, and let the mixer kneed it for 10 minutes.
When done kneading, remove the dough hook. Pull out the dough onto the counter, and
kneed it together into a big smooth ball. Let is rest and rise for 45 minutes in the bowl.

Take up the dough; divide it into 20 equal buns, or 3 equal pieces to create round loaves.
Let the breads/buns rest for 15-20 minutes covered

Turn on the oven to 425/450° F.

Beat the egg, and brush the breads/buns, sprinkle sea salt and thyme over the breads.
For loaves: bake it in 425 degree oven, for 17-19 minutes.
For buns: bake it in 450 degree oven for 12 minutes.

Let the breads/buns rest then sheet pan for 5 minutes then move them to a wire rack and let
them finish cooling off.

.

White Bread (Use for Sandwich Cakes)

2 tbsp dry instant SAF™ yeast
2 cups of milk
2 oz butter, melted
1 tsp salt
2 tsp sugar
1 egg
1 lb 10 oz unbleached bread flour

Garnish
Blue poppy seeds
Sesame seeds
1 egg, for egg wash

Oven temperature:
For 2 loaves
Gas or Electric Oven: 400° F
Second Lowest Rack 20 minutes
Or for Sandwich Cakes
Two 9-inches round cake pans,
"spring form" preferably.
Bake for 25-30 minutes in the oven.

Melt the butter, add the milk. The temperature should be warm, but not hot.
Place the yeast in the mixing bowl add sugar; pour the liquid over the yeast.

Mix the salt with the flour, add all the dry ingredients to the wet ingredients, and let the mixer kneed it for 10 minutes.
When done kneading, remove the dough hook. Pull out the dough onto the counter, and kneed it together into a big smooth ball, divided it to 2 pieces. Let is rest and rise for 45 minutes in the bowl.

For loaves:
Prepare two loaf pans and dress them with parchment paper.
Divide it into total of 4 equal pieces. Roll the dough pieces to approx 12-14 inches long.
Grab two of the dough pieces and twist them together. Place them in the prepared pans.
Let the breads rest for 20 minutes covered.
Make the egg wash and brush them, sprinkle either sesame seed or blue poppy seed on top.

For rounds for Sandwich Cakes:
Dress two 9-inches round cake pans, "spring form" preferably with parchment paper.
Kneed the two pieces of dough, and pat it out so it fits the cake pans, let the rounds rest
For 20 minutes covered. NO EGG WASH ON THESE ROUNDS

Bake the loaves in the preheated oven 400°F for 20 minutes.

Bake the rounds in the preheated oven 400°F for 25-30 minutes.

Sundried Tomato & Black Olive Bread

2 tbsp dry instant SAF™ yeast
2 cup warm water
¼ cup olive oil
3 tbsp sugar
1 tbsp salt
2 tbsp sweet dry basil
1 tbsp dry oregano
1 shallot onion, small and finely chopped
2.6 oz chopped sun dried tomatoes in oil + 1/8 cup of the oil from the tomatoes
2 oz black olives, chopped
1 lb 10 oz unbleached flour

Oven temperature:
Gas or Electric Oven: 400° F
Second Lowest Rack 35-40 minutes

Put the dry instant yeast in the mixing bowl and add the sugar.

Pour the water mixture over the yeast and sugar; add the olive oil, the sundried tomatoes, + 1/8 cup of oil from the tomatoes. Whisk together the wet ingredients.

Mix 1 lb and 10 oz of flour with the salt, basil and oregano, add that to the wet ingredients.

Attach the dough hook, and let it knead for 10 minutes.

When done kneading, remove the dough hook. Pull out the dough onto the counter, and kneed it together into a big smooth ball. Brush the dough with olive oil and let it rest covered for 1 ½ hour.

Turn on the oven to 400° F.

After resting, pull out the dough on to the counter, and divide the dough into three equal parts. Work the dough and kneed it together in to three rounds.

Place the rounds on a parchment paper lined baking sheet; make diagonal cuts on the top of each bread. Brush the breads with olive oil and sprinkle coarse kosher salt on top.

Let them rise for 15 minutes uncovered.

Bake the bread for 35-40 minutes.

When they come out of the oven let them rest for 5 minutes then move them to a wire rack and let them finish cooling off.

Sunflower Seed Buns
(great for sandwiches if you run a deli or sandwich/soup shop)

2 tbsp dry instant SAF™ yeast
23 fl oz (700 ml) water
1 ¼ cup sunflower seeds
12.7 oz instant oatmeal
2 tsp herb salt of your choice French or Italian
1 lb 7oz unbleached bread flour

Egg wash and topping:
1 egg
½ tsp water
3 tsp herb salt
¼ cup sunflower seeds

Put the dry instant yeast in the mixing bowl pour the warm water over it.
Add the sunflower seeds and the oatmeal. Stir it all together, let it rest for 5 minutes.

Mix the flour with the herb salt. Add the flour to the sunflowers seed and oatmeal mix.
Attach the dough hook, and let it knead for 10 minutes.

When done kneading, remove the dough hook. Pull out the dough onto the counter, and kneed it together into a big smooth ball. Place the dough back into the bowl, and let it rest and rise for 45 minutes.

After resting, pull out the dough on to the counter, and work the dough, kneed it together. Divide the dough into 20 equal parts. Create round shaped buns, and place them on greased flour dusted sheet pans.
Let the buns rise uncovered for 15 minutes.

Preheat the oven to 450° F.
Make the egg wash, mix egg, and water. Brush the buns, and sprinkle sunflower seed and herb salt on top.

Bake the buns for 12-14 minutes. When the buns come out of the oven let them rest on the baking sheet for 5 minutes then move them to a wire rack and let them finish cooling off.

Foccacia Bread w/ Sun Dried Tomatoes, Parmesan and Mozzarella Cheese

(great for sandwiches if you run a deli or sandwich/soup shop)

Oven temperature:
Gas or Electric Oven: 425° F
Second Lowest Rack 13-15 minutes

2 3/4 cups all-purpose flour
1 tsp salt
1 tsp white sugar
1 tbsp instant SAF™ yeast
1 tsp garlic powder
1 tsp oregano
1/2 tsp dried thyme
1/2 tsp dried basil
½ cup shredded sundried tomatoes in oil
1 dash ground black pepper
1 tbsp vegetable oil
1 cup water
2 tbsp olive oil
2 tbsp grated parmesan cheese
1 1/2 cups shredded mozzarella cheese

In large bowl, stir together flour, salt, sugar, yeast, garlic powder, oregano, thyme, basil, and black pepper.
Mix in vegetable oil and water.

When dough has pulled together, turn out onto lightly floured surface and knead until smooth and elastic.

Lightly oil a large bowl, place dough in bowl, and turn to coat with oil.

Cover with damp cloth and let rise in warm place 25 minutes.
Preheat oven to 425° F degrees.

Punch dough down, place on greased baking sheet. Pat dough into 1/2-inch thick rectangle (doesn't have to be perfect). Using your knuckle, make indentations in the dough about 1/2-inch apart, then prick dough with fork.

Brush top with olive oil, then sprinkle with shredded sundried tomatoes, Parmesan and mozzarella cheese. Bake for 13-15 minutes until golden brown.

Rye Bread w/Anise & Fennel & Quark

2 tbsp dry instant SAF ™ yeast
2 cup warm water
2 oz butter, melted
½ cup Lyle's golden syrup or Grandma's original molasses
8.8 oz (250gr.) Low Fat Quark
1.5 lb white bread flour
1 lb dark rye flour (can be replaced with whole wheat flour if you prefer)
½ tbsp ground fennel
½ tbsp ground anise
2 tsp salt

Put the dry instant yeast in the mixing bowl.

Melt the butter, pour the water over it. Pour the water mixture over the yeast add syrup, and quark. Whisk together the wet ingredients.

Mix the flours; add the salt, fennel, and anise into the flour, mix again.

Attach the dough hook, and let it knead for 10 minutes.

When done kneading, remove the dough hook. Pull out the dough onto the counter, and kneed it together into a big smooth ball.

Let is rest and rise for 45 minutes.

Divide the dough into two equal parts. Kneed it together in to a loaf.

Have two loaf pans ready, and lined with parchment paper, place the loaves in the pans. Let them rise for 20-30 minutes.

Turn on the oven 350° F.

After rising place the loaf pans in the second lowest part of the oven. Bake for 40 minutes.

Let the bread rest for 10 minutes in the pan, and then remove them out of the pan then move them to a wire rack and let them finish cooling off.

Lazy Graham Squares

(great for sandwiches if you run a deli or sandwich/soup shop)

18 units

2 tbsp dry instant SAF™ yeast
2 1/8 cups of warm water
1 oz butter, soft
1 ½ tsp salt
2 tbsp honey or Lyles Golden Syrup
8.8 oz low fat quark
3.9 oz graham flour
1 lb 8 oz white bread flour

Put the dry instant yeast in the mixing bowl.

Pour the warm water over it, stir, and dissolve the yeast. Add the softened butter, syrup, and quark. Whisk together the wet ingredients.
Mix the flours; add the salt to the flour. Add the flour to the wet mixture.

Attach the dough hook, and let it knead for 10 minutes.

When done kneading, remove the dough hook. Pull out the dough onto the counter, and kneed it together into a big smooth ball.

Let is rest and rise in the bowl for 40 minutes.

Remove the dough after rising.

Roll out the dough to size that will fit a half sheet pan.

Line the half sheet pan with a parchment paper, and place the rolled out dough on it.

Cut the dough into squares with a sharp knife (6 x 3) in the half sheet pan. Let the dough rest for 20-30 minutes covered.

Turn on the oven to 425° F.

When the dough is done rising, dust the top of the bread with some graham flour. Bake in the middle of the rack for 15 minutes. Let the bread cool off on a wire rack covered.

Herb Bread w/ Cottage Cheese

2 tbsp dry instant SAF™ yeast
2 oz butter, melted
¾ cup (200ml) milk
1/3 cup Lyles Golden Syrup
2 tsp salt
7 oz cottage cheese
5 tbsp freshly chopped basil
5 tbsp freshly chopped parsley, curly or flat leaf
7.7 oz graham flour
13.6 oz unbleached bread flour

Egg wash:
1 egg
½ tsp water
Coarse Kosher Salt

Oven temperature:
Gas or Electric Oven:
Start temperature 400° F

As soon as you put the bread in the oven, lower it to 350° F
Second Lowest Rack, 20-25 minutes

Put the dry instant yeast in the mixing bowl.

Melt the butter, pour the milk over it. Pour the milk and butter mixture over the yeast add syrup, basil, parsley, and cottage cheese. Whisk together the wet ingredients.

Mix the flours; add the salt, mix again.

Add all the flour to the wet ingredients, attach the dough hook, and let it knead for 10 minutes. The dough will be a little bit damp, that is ok.

When done kneading, remove the dough hook. Pull out the dough onto the counter, sprinkle a little bit flour on the counter, and kneed it together into a big smooth ball.

Let is rest and rise covered in the bowl for 45 minutes.

After resting, pull out the dough on to the counter, and divide the dough into three equal parts. Work the dough and kneed it together in to two smaller rounds, or one large round.

Place the bread on a parchment paper lined baking sheet; let it rise again for 20 minutes.

Preheat the oven to 400° F.

Mix egg and water for the egg wash, brush the bread with the egg wash, and sprinkle some coarse kosher salt.

Put the bread in the oven, and immediately turn down the heat to 350° F.

Bake the bread for 20-25 minutes, until the bread feels hollow. You can check by knocking under the bread and then you will hear a hollow sound.

Let the bread rest for 5 minutes on the baking sheet then move them to a wire rack and let them finish cooling off.

Swedish Wortbread (Svenskt Vörtbröd, *Christmas bread*)

2 tbsp dry Instant SAF™ yeast
2 oz butter
¾ (200 ml) cup Julmust (Swedish Christmas drink) or Dr Pepper™
1 bottle porter, 12 fl oz (330 ml)
8.8 oz (250 gr.) low fat quark
1/3 cup Lyles Golden Syrup or Grandma's Original Molasses
2 tsp salt
2 tsp ground ginger
2 tbsp ground orange peel
1/8 tsp ground cloves
2 oz raisins
1.5 lb white bread flour
1 lb rye flour

Put the dry instant yeast in the mixing bowl.

Melt the butter; pour porter and julmust or Dr. Pepper™ over it. Pour the butter and porter mixture over the yeast add syrup, and quark. Whisk together the wet ingredients.

Mix the flours; add the salt, ginger, cloves, raisins into the flour, mix again.

Attach the dough hook, and let it knead for 10 minutes.

When done kneading, remove the dough hook. Pull out the dough onto the counter, and kneed it together into a big smooth ball.

Let is rest and rise for 45 minutes.

Divide the dough into two equal parts. Kneed it together in to a loaf.

Have two loaf pans ready, and lined with parchment paper, place the loaves in the pans. Let them rise for 20-30 minutes.

Turn on the oven 350° F.

After rising place the loaf pans in the second lowest part of the oven. Bake for 40 minutes.

Melt some butter in a pot. When the bread comes out of the oven, brush the loaves with the butter.

Let the bread rest for 10 minutes in the pan, and then remove them out of the pan then move them to a wire rack and let them finish cooling off.

NOTES

Muffins

Gingerbread Muffins

3.52 oz (100 g) butter, softened
1 cup brown sugar
2 egg
5 fl oz(150 ml) buttermilk
5.8 oz (155 gr.) unbleached all purpose flour
1 tbsp cinnamon
1 tsp cloves
1 tsp ginger
1 tsp baking soda

Yield 20 muffins

Preheat the oven to 350°F.

Attach the paddle attachment to the mixer. Place the butter in the mixing bowl, add the sugar, and mix it until it is completely incorporated.

Mix the flour with the spices and the baking soda in a bowl, set a side.

Add one egg at the time while mixing the butter. Add the buttermilk.

Last, mix in flour mixture, don't over mix.

Use normal size muffin pan, 12 muffins in a pan. Dress the muffin pan with paper cups.

Bake the muffins in the middle of the oven, for 20 minutes.

Oatmeal & Cardamom Muffin

Oven temperature:
Gas or Electric Oven: 350° F
Middle Rack, 25 minutes

2 egg
6 oz granulated sugar
2 oz melted butter
5.8 oz unbleached all purpose flour
1 1/2 tsp baking powder
½ cup buttermilk

Filling:
1/3 cup (100 ml) melted butter
1 tsp vanilla sugar
1/8 + 1 tbsp granulated sugar
4.2 oz instant oatmeal
2 tsp ground cardamom

Yield 12 normal size or 6 jumbo size

Preheat the oven to 350°F.

Attach the whisk attachment to your mixer.

Place egg and sugar in the bowl, and whisk it pale and fluffy.

Mix the flour with baking powder.

Stir in (do not whisk) flour mixture, buttermilk, and melted butter.

Use normal size (yield 12) or jumbo size muffin pan (yield 6). Dress the muffin pan with paper cups, and fill the cups.

Make the filling, melt the butter mix in vanilla sugar, sugar, oatmeal, and cardamom.

Divide the filling on top each muffin (12 or 6).

Bake the muffins in middle rack for 25 minutes.

Bailey's™ Cup Cake Muffin

Oven temperature:
Gas or Electric Oven: 350° F
Middle Rack, 20 minutes

3 eggs
1 cup granulated sugar
1 tsp vanilla sugar
3.52 oz (100 g) butter
1/3 cup milk
1 1/3 cup unbleached all purpose flour
2 tsp baking powder
1/8 tsp salt
4-5 tbsp Bailey's™

Frosting:
7 oz (200 gr.) Philadelphia Cheese
2 cups powdered sugar, add more if needed.
1-2 tbsp Bailey's™

Decoration:
Fresh half cut strawberries
Shaved chocolate

Yield 12 normal muffins

Preheat the oven to 350°F.

Attach the whisk attachment to your mixer.
Place egg and sugar in the bowl, and whisk it pale and fluffy.

Mix the flour with baking powder and salt in a bowl, set a side.

Melt the butter and pour the milk over the butter. Add the flour mixture, and mix lightly. Add the Bailey's™.

Use normal size muffin pan, 12 muffins in a pan. Dress the muffin pan with paper cups. Bake the muffins in the middle of the oven, for 20 minutes. Let the muffin cool down before frosting them.

Mix the Philadelphia cheese with powdered sugar, add the Bailey's™, If you need more sugar add more sugar; the frosting should be thick, and not runny.

Decorate with cutting the strawberries in half, and shave some dark or milk chocolate over the top.

Blueberry & Raspberry Muffins w/ Almond Paste

5.3 oz (150 gr.) Almond Paste
9.7 oz unbleached all purpose flour
3 oz granulated sugar
1 tsp baking powder
1/2 tsp baking soda
1/2 tsp salt
2 tsp vanilla sugar
5.3 oz softened butter
2 eggs
2/3 cup (150 ml) milk
1 ¼ cup frozen blueberries and raspberries
Sliced almonds for garnish

Yield 6 jumbo muffins or 12 normal size muffins

Preheat the oven to 350°F.

Mix the dry ingredients in a large bowl, set a side.
Grate the almond paste on a grating box.
Attach the paddle attachment to the mixer. Place the butter in the mixing bowl, add the almond paste, and mix it until it is completely incorporated and fluffy.

Add the eggs, one a time, and lastly the milk.

Pour the egg mixture over the dry ingredients and stir it all together. Fold in the frozen berries into the batter.
Dress the muffin pan with paper cups. Divide the batter among the cups. Sprinkle the sliced almonds on top of each muffin.

Bake in the oven for 15-20 minutes. Cooking time is depending on what size of muffin you are making.

Blackberry & White Chocolate Muffin

Oven temperature:
Gas or Electric Oven: 350° F
Middle Rack, 15-20 minutes

¾ cup granulated sugar
3 eggs
1 tsp baking powder
1 tsp vanilla sugar
1 cup unbleached all purpose flour
3.52 oz (100 gr.) melted butter
3.52 oz chopped white chocolate
1 ¼ cup frozen or fresh Blackberries

Yield 12 normal size muffins

Preheat the oven to 350°F.

Attach the whisk attachment to your mixer.
Place egg and sugar in the bowl, and whisk it pale and fluffy.

Mix the flour with baking powder and vanilla sugar in a bowl, pour that into the egg mixture.
Melt the butter and stir (not whisk) it into the mixture.
Stir in the chopped white chocolate.

Dress the muffin pan with paper cups. Divide the batter among the cups.

Stick down a couple of large blackberries in to each muffin.

Bake in the oven for 15-20 minutes.

Soft Cakes

Tosca Cake

Oven temperature:
Gas or Electric Oven: 425° F
Second lowest rack,
15-20 minutes

Cake:
3.52 oz butter
¾ cup milk
4 eggs
12.3 oz granualted sugar
11.6 oz unbleached all purpose flour
1 tbsp baking powder
1 tbsp vanilla sugar
2 tsp almond extract

Tosca Topping:
5.3 oz butter
1.5 oz granulated sugar
7.4 oz Lyle's golden syrup
3 tbsp unbleached all purpose flour
3 tbsp water
7 oz sliced almonds

Preheat the oven to 425°F degrees.

Place two parchment papers on a half sheet pan, covering each other.

  Melt the butter, add the milk. Use a mixing bowl and attach the whisk attachment and whip the egg and sugar, white and fluffy.
  Mix the flour, vanilla sugar, and baking powder, fold that into the batter with the melted butter and milk at the same time.
  Pour it onto the baking sheet and even it out with a spatula. Bake in the oven for 12 minutes.

Meanwhile make the Tosca topping.

  Melt the butter in a pot; add sugar, Lyle's golden syrup, flour, and water. Let it all simmer together for 5 minutes. Add the sliced almonds to the mix.

  Take out the cake after 12 minutes, and spread the Tosca over the cake, put it back into the oven on upper rack. Let the cake finish baking for 8 minutes, until the Tosca is bubbling, and have a nice amber color.
  Take out the cake and let it cool off before cutting into it.

Chocolate Cinnamon Ginger Cake w/ Tjinuski Toffee

1/2 cup (4 oz) butter, softened, plus more for
pan
1/2 cup unsweetened Dutch process cocoa
powder, plus more for dusting
1/2 cup molasses, black strap, or Grandma's
Original Molasses
3/4 cup packed light-brown sugar
2 large eggs
¼ cup water
¼ cup whole milk
1 cup all-purpose flour
¾ tsp baking soda

½ tsp coarse salt
½ tsp ground ginger
1½ tsp ground cinnamon
¼ cup chocolate chips (optional)

_____

Tjinuski Toffee:
1 ¼ cup heavy cream
¾ cup sugar
1/3 cup Lyles Golden Syrup
1 tbsp butter
1 tbsp vanilla sugar

Oven temperature:
Gas or Electric Oven: 325° F
Second lowest rack, 30 minutes

Preheat oven to 325° F degrees.

Butter a 9-inch Bundt pan. Dust with
cocoa powder, and tap out excess, put a
side.

Put butter, molasses, brown sugar, and 1/4
cup water in a medium saucepan over
medium-low heat. Cook, stirring
constantly, until butter has melted.

Transfer mixture to a large bowl. Let it
cool for 5 minutes.

Add eggs, milk, to the molasses mixture;
whisk to combine. Stir together flour,
cocoa powder, baking soda, salt, ground
ginger, and ground cinnamon with a
balloon whisk into a medium bowl.

Gently fold the flour mixture into the
molasses mixture until just combined.

Pour batter into prepared pan. *(Optional:
sprinkle the chocolate chip over the cake)*
Bake cake until a cake tester inserted into
center comes out clean, about 30 minutes.
Let cake cool completely in pan on a wire
rack. Invert cake, and unmold onto a cake
stand or a large serving platter.

Tjinuski:
Mix cream, sugar, syrup, into a heavy
sauce pan. Cook the toffee for 20-30
minutes on medium heat. When the toffee
has thickened and it has a look of golden
brown color. Take it off the heat, and stir
in the butter. Let the toffee cool, add the
vanilla sugar.
Drizzle the toffee in a back a forward
motion over the cake. Serve immediately
with some whipped cream.

Pumpkin Spice Cake w/ Cranberries

Oven temperature:
Gas or Electric Oven: 350° F
Middle rack, 30 minutes

11 oz cake flour
2 tsp baking powder
1 tsp baking soda
1 tsp ground ginger
1 ½ tsp ground cinnamon
¼ tsp round allspice
¼ tsp ground cloves
½ tsp salt

2 cups sugar
1 cup canola oil or vegetable oil

4 large eggs

15 oz pureed pumpkin from can
1 teaspoon vanilla extract
Grated peel of 1 orange

6 tbsp cranberries

Yield 3 loaf pans

Preheat oven to 350°F.

Prepare 3 loaf pans and dress them with parchment paper.

Mix together all the dry ingredients.

Attach the paddle attachment to the mixer. Place the sugar and oil in the mixing bowl; blend it well, around 2 minutes. Add eggs 1 at a time, beating well after each addition.

Add pumpkin, orange peel and vanilla; beat until blended.

Gradually add dry ingredients; beat just until incorporated. Divide batter between prepared pans; smooth top with spatula. Sprinkle the cranberries on top of each cake, and use a fork to swirl it in to the batter.

Bake cakes about 30 minutes. Cool for 10 minutes, then remove the cakes from the loaf pans and let them finish resting onto wire racks to cool completely.

Carrot Cake w/ Cream Cheese Frosting

Oven temperature:
Gas or Electric Oven: 325° F
Second Lowest rack, 60 minutes

Cake:
2 cups of unbleached flour
2 cups of sugar
2 tbsp cinnamon
2 tbsp baking soda
1 tbsp baking powder
1 tbsp allspice
2 tsp pumpkin spice
1 cup chopped toasted walnuts
1/2 cup raisins

1 small can crushed pineapple
2 cups fine grated carrots
3 large eggs
1 cup oil
1 tbsp Mexican vanilla extract

Frosting:
12 oz Philadelphia Cream Cheese
6 oz softened butter
24 oz powdered sugar
1 1/2 tbsp vanilla extract

Turn on the oven to 325°F.

Mix all the wet ingredients in the mixer with the paddle attachment.
Add all the dry ingredients.
Mix until everything is incorporated, don't over mix, the risk for making the cake tough if mixing it too long.
Grease 13 x 11 pan all around the edges; pour the batter into the pan.
Bake in 325°F degree oven for 1 hr.

Frosting:
Beat the cream cheese until it is soft and airy. Add the softened butter and vanilla, mix it up together.
Add slowly the powdered sugar, until it is all incorporated, and airy.
Frost the cake after it has cooled off.

Lemoncello™ Cake w/ Blueberries

Oven temperature:
Gas or Electric Oven: 325° F
Middle rack, 75 minutes

1 cup butter, room temperature, plus more for baking pan
2 cups granulated sugar
4 large eggs, room temperature
3 cups all-purpose flour
1/2 teaspoon baking soda
1/2 teaspoon salt
1 cup buttermilk
Grate lemon peel from 2 large lemons
2 1/2 tablespoons Lemoncello™
1 cup dried blueberries
1/2 cup powdered sugar
1-2 tbsp lemon juice,

Preheat the oven to 325 degrees.
Place on the middle rack. Dress two loaf pans with parchment paper.

Attach the paddle attachment to the mixer. Place the butter and sugar in the bowl, and cream butter and sugar light and fluffy on medium speed for 3 minutes.

Add eggs, one at a time, beating well after each addition, and scraping down the sides of the bowl.

Place the flour, baking soda, and salt into a medium bowl and stir it up with a balloon whisk. Add the flour mixture to the butter mixture in three additions, alternating with buttermilk, and beginning and ending with the flour mixture. Stir in lemoncello™ and zest.

Pour batter into the prepared pan, smoothing the top with a rubber spatula.
Sprinkle ½ cup of dried blueberries on each cake. Use a fork to swirl it into the cakes.

Bake in the oven for 75 minutes, until a tester inserted into the center comes out clean and the cake has begun to pull away from the sides of the pan. Let the loaf pans rest on a wire rack to cool for 10 minutes.

Meanwhile, prepare the glaze: In a small bowl, whisk together confectioners' sugar, lemon juice, set aside.
Remove the cakes from the pans, and drizzle the glaze in a back and forward motion on top of the cakes.

Banana Cake (no nuts)

Ingredients:

2/3 cup + 4 tbsp granulated sugar
2 large eggs
3.5 oz melted butter
2 regular size mashed bananas
6.3 oz all purpose flour
1 ½ tsp baking powder
1 tsp baking soda
2 tsp vanilla sugar or extract
6 tbsp cream

Oven temperature:
Gas or Electric Oven: 350° F
Second lowest rack, 35 minutes

Preheat up the oven to 350°F degrees.

Grease and flour a rectangular or round (1 ½ qt) baking pan.

Melt the butter in the microwave for 1 minute, add the cream, let it cool.

Whip the eggs and sugar white and fluffy.

Mix the dry ingredients, and fold it into the egg batter.

Add the butter/cream, and fold that in.

Last but not least fold in the mashed bananas.

Pour the batter into the pan and bake it in the oven for 35 minutes.

Take it out and let the cake rest in the pan. Before serving, dust some powdered sugar on top.

Zucchini Cake

¾ cup vegetable oil
1 2/3 cup brown sugar
1 2/3 cup fine shredded zucchini
4 large eggs
14.55 oz unbleached all purpose flour
1 tsp baking powder
1 tsp baking soda
2 tsp cinnamon
1 tsp salt
¼ cup crème fraiche
1/3 cup coarsely chopped walnuts

Oven temperature:
Gas or Electric Oven: 350° F
Lowest rack, 60 minutes
2 pans, size 1 ½ qt each

Preheat the oven to 350° F.

Butter two 1 ½ qt pans. Dust with flour, and tap out excess, put a side.

Attach the paddle attachment to the mixer. Place the oil and sugar in the bowl, whip it for 2 minutes. Add the shredded zucchini, stir. Add one egg at the time, incorporate well after each.

Mix the flour in a bowl with the baking powder, baking soda, cinnamon, and salt.
Add the flour mixture to the zucchini mixture, alternating with crème fraiche and beginning and ending with the flour mixture. (*flour amount varies depending on the 'juiciness of the zucchini, if more flour is needed only add 1/8 cup at the most*)

Fold in the walnuts.

Pour the batter into the two prepared pans, bake on the lowest rack in the oven for 60 minutes.

Potato Cake w/ Chocolate

A cake without flour? Yes it is possible.
The cake should be a little sticky when it is
done, that is when it is at its best.
Whipped Cream is a great with the cake.

3-4 not all too big potatoes
3.52 oz butter
2 large eggs
1/3 cup sugar
1 tbsp vanilla sugar
4 tbsp unsweetened cocoa
½ tsp salt

Powdered sugar for dusting

Oven temperature:
Gas or Electric Oven: 300° F Second
Lowest rack, 30-40 minutes
1 pan, 8 inches in diameter

Butter one 8-inch pan. Dust with flour, and tap out excess, put a side.

Peel, cook the potatoes. Then let them through a potato ricer.

Melt the butter, mix in all the ingredients into the butter.

Bake the cake in the oven for 30-40 minutes on the second lowest rack.

Chocolate Cake w/ Coconut & Butterscotch

Oven temperature:
Gas or Electric Oven: 350° F
Second lowest rack, 17-22
minutes

7 oz butter
4 eggs
2 ½ cup granulated sugar
1 cup + 4 tbsp flour
8 tbsp cocoa
2 tsp vanilla
1 tsp salt
3.4 oz fine chopped dark chocolate (at least 60 % cocoa)
Fine shredded coconut to the spring form
Approx. 6.8 oz butterscotch chips

Preheat the oven to 350°F.

Butter the 10 x 15 jelly roll pan, and sprinkle shredded coconut to cover the inside.

Melt the butter in a pot, set a side.

Whisk together egg, sugar, vanilla.

Stir in flour, cocoa, and salt.

Add the melted butter, whisk together everything thorough.

Finely chop the dark chocolate, and fold it into the batter.

Pour all the batter into the pan and bake it in the oven for 17-22 minutes. Test the cake with a wooden pick to check the readiness of the cake. When the batter does not stick to it and it comes out clean it is done. (It will still be sticky and chocolaty)

Take out the cake and let it rest for 2 minutes before you sprinkle the butterscotch chips onto the cake, it will melt; spread the butterscotch carefully over the cake. Let it cool.

Cut your individual pieces as it fits you and your crowd.

Chocolate Toffee Cake w/ Nuts

1 oz almonds
2 oz walnuts
2 oz hazelnuts
5.3 oz sugar
2 eggs
2.7 oz flour
1 tsp baking powder
1 tsp vanilla sugar
1/3 cup heavy whipping cream

Chocolate Toffee Cream:
4.4 oz sugar
1 tbsp unsweetened cocoa
2.7 oz butter
1/3 cup heavy whipping cream

Preheat the oven to 350° F.

Butter one 9-inch springform pan. Dust with flour, and tap out excess, put a side.

Grind the nuts; you can us your food processor, and the knife blade. Be careful to not grind too long so that the oils are starting to extract.

Attach the whisk attachment to the mixer. Place the eggs and sugar in the mixing bowl. Whisk the egg and sugar, white and fluffy.

Mix the flour, baking powder, vanilla sugar and the nuts in a separate bowl.

Fold in the dry ingredients with a balloon whisk, add the cream last. Pour the batter into the pan.
Bake the cake in the oven for 30 minutes.

While the cake is baking make the chocolate toffee cream.
Melt the butter, and mix in the rest of the ingredients. Stir while it is cooking, it should cook until it has thickened.

When the cake has cooled off, spread the chocolate toffee cream over the cake, and let it run down the sides.
Serve the cake with a dollop of whipped cream.

Genoise, Simple Yellow Cake

Oven temperature:
Gas or Electric Oven: 350° F
Middle rack, 25-30 minutes

3 large eggs
3 large egg yolks
2 tsp vanilla sugar or extract
1/8 tsp salt
½ cup sugar
½ cup of all purpose flour
¼ cup cornstarch

Preheat the oven to 350° F.

Butter one 9-inch springform pan; place a disk of parchment paper on the bottom. Dust with flour, and tap out excess, put a side (or line a half sheet (baking sheet) with a parchment paper, and grease the side).

Place a saucepan with water on the stove and bring it to a simmer.

Mix the eggs, egg yolks, vanilla and salt in the mixing bowl. Whisk by hand with a balloon whisk, add the sugar gradually.
Place the mixing bowl over the simmering water, whisk with the balloon whisk until the egg mixture has reached the temperature of 115° F (45°C).

Attach the whisk attachment to the mixer. Place the mixing bowl, and start whisking the egg mix white and fluffy on medium high speed. Whisk for 4 minutes. The volume has not tripled.

Mix the flour and cornstarch in a separate bowl, mix the flours with a balloon whisk.

Fold in 1/3 of the flour with a rubber spatula; make sure you dig down in the bowl every time you pass through so no lumps of flours are left there. Add half of the remainder flour folding until it has dissolved; add the rest of the flour as previously directed.
Pour the batter in the prepared pan, (or baking sheet) smooth on top.

Bake in the oven for 25-30 minutes. (15-20 minutes for baking sheet pan)
When the cake is out of the oven, immediately unmold it from the springform and let it cool on a rack. The cake should cool with the top side up.

Nutrition (per serving/ 10 servings): **118.6 calories**; 24% calories from fat; 3.1g total fat; 136.5mg cholesterol; 57.5mg sodium; 35.9mg potassium; 21.2g carbohydrates; 0.2g fiber; 10.2g sugar; 21.0g net carbs; 3.7g protein.

Jelly Roll Cakes

Brownie

Traditional Jelly Roll

Oven temperature:
Gas or Electric Oven: 450° F
Middle rack, 5 minutes

3 eggs
6.1 oz sugar
4 oz unbleached all purpose flour
2 tsp baking powder
3 tbsp + 1 tsp milk

Filling:
¾ cup jam, preserves, or apple sauce

Preheat the oven to 450° F degree.

Line a jelly roll pan with parchment paper. (Approx 11 x 15)

Attach the whisk attachment to the mixer. Place the eggs and sugar in the mixing bowl and whisk it until eggs and sugars are yellow pale and fluffy.

Mix the baking powder with the flour, and fold that into the egg mixture. Add the liquid and fold into the batter.

Pour the batter onto the baking sheet, and bake it in the oven for 5-6 minutes.

Meanwhile grab another parchment paper and line it onto the counter, and sprinkle granulated sugar all over the parchment paper.

Take out the cake and flip it onto the sugared parchment paper cake side down.
(Easy way of doing it, is to grasp the cake by the corners and lift it off the baking sheet and place it onto the sugared parchment paper with the cake side down.)

Remove the paper, *if you have a hard time, use some ice cold water and brush the water with a pastry brush on top of the paper and roll it off as you brush.*

Spread the filling on top of the cake and roll it up from the shortest side. Wrap it up in the parchment paper, and let it cool down before cutting into it.

Jelly Roll Pastry w/ Fruit

Make a "Traditional Jelly Roll" bottom according to the instructions on page 48.

1 batch of Traditional Jelly Roll

Filling:
2 ½ cup heavy whipping cream
¾ cup of berries, blueberry, raspberry, blackberry, strawberry, huckleberry etc.
3 tbsp granulated sugar

Garnish:
Whipped heavy cream
1 ½ cup of berries

Make a "Traditional Jelly Roll" bottom according to the instructions on page 48.
Do not spread any jam on it when it is warm; only remove the parchment paper off it.
Let the cake cool off under a second baking sheet, this will ensure that the cake does not crack.

Whip the cream. Mash the berries. Mix the berries with the sugar, and fold it gently into 2/3 of the whipped cream.

Spread the filling on to the cooled off cake, and roll it up from the short side.
Cut the jelly roll into thick pieces; turn the jelly roll piece up with the cut surface up.
Garnish with whipped cream, and berries on top.

Dream Roll

Oven temperature:
Gas or Electric Oven: 450° F
Middle rack, 5 minutes

3 eggs
4.6 oz sugar
2.1 oz potato starch flour
1 tsp baking powder
2 tbsp unsweetened cocoa powder

Filling:
3.5 oz butter a little bit soft (do not let the butter sit out over night)
¾ cup powdered sugar
2 tsp vanilla sugar
1 egg yolk

Preheat the oven to 450° F degree.

Line a jelly roll pan (approx 11 x 15) with parchment paper; use come cooking spray to spray the parchment paper lightly.

Attach the whisk attachment to the mixer. Place the eggs and sugar in the mixing bowl and whisk it until eggs and sugars are yellow pale and fluffy.

Mix the baking powder with the flour, and cocoa and fold that into the egg mixture.
Pour the batter onto the baking sheet, and bake it in the oven for 5-6 minutes.

Meanwhile grab another parchment paper and line it onto the counter, and sprinkle granulated sugar all over the parchment paper.

Take out the cake and flip it onto the sugared parchment paper cake side down.
(Easy way of doing it, is to grasp the cake by the corners and lift it off the baking sheet and place it onto the sugared parchment paper with the cake side down.)

Remove the paper. *(If you have a hard time, use some ice cold water and brush the water with a pastry brush on top of the paper and roll it off as you brush.)* Let the jelly roll cool off.

Mix the butter, sugar smooth. Stir in the vanilla sugar. Last stir in the egg yolk.
Spread the filling on top of the cake and roll it up from the shortest side. Wrap it up in the parchment paper, and let it cake sit in a cold spot before cutting into it.

Love Munch Brownies

Oven temperature:
Gas or Electric Oven: 425° F
Middle rack, 10-15 minutes

Cake:
10 tbsp butter
3 eggs
1 1/4 cup Sugar
2/3 cup milk
1 1/4 cup white flour
3 tbsp cocoa
1 tbsp baking powder
1 tbsp vanilla sugar or extract

Chocolate Topping Sauce:
7 tbsp butter
3/4 cup heavy cream
4 tbsp sugar
2 tsp white flour
2 tbsp cocoa

Servings: 10-12 depending on size

Cake:

Preheat the oven to 425°F degrees.

Whisk egg and sugar yellow pale and fluffy. Stir in slowly the butter, milk alternating the dry ingredients.

Pour the cake mix into a 9 x 13 deep-dish pan lined with parchment paper. Bake in the oven for 10-15 minutes.

Let the cake cool off before pouring the chocolate sauce onto it.

Chocolate Topping Sauce:

Melt the butter and mix in the rest of the ingredients. Simmer the sauce slowly for 5-7 min until the sauce has thickened.

Pour the sauce over the cake and garnish with coconut flakes, nut of your choice.

Suggestion: Cut a square, put it on a plate, heat it up in the microwave oven for 10 sec, and add a scoop of vanilla ice cream and some hot fudge on top of the ice-cream.

NOTES

Small Cookies

Meringues

Dreams

7 oz butter
18 oz granulated sugar
2 tsp vanilla sugar
¾ cup vegetable oil
1 tsp baking ammonia
1 tsp baking soda
15.52 oz unbleached all purpose flour

Yield: 86

Preheat the oven to 300° F.

Attach the paddle attachment to the mixer. Place the butter in the mixing bowl, add the sugar, and vanilla sugar. Mix it until the butter gets creamy. Add the oil gradually to the butter mix.

Mix the baking ammonia and baking soda to the flour, and pour the flour into the mix. Mix it all well until combined.

Use the ice cream scooper (¾ oz) to scoop out the dough on parchment paper covered sheets.

Bake in the oven for 20 min on 300 degree F

Toffee Cookie

Oven temperature:
Gas or Electric Oven: 325° F
Second Lowest rack, 17-20
minutes

1 stick of butter
1/3 cup of granulate sugar
1 tbsp light syrup or Lyle's Golden Syrup
1 cup of flour
1 tsp baking powder
1 tbsp vanilla sugar

Yield approx: 40

Preheat the oven to 325° F.
Mix together all the ingredients in a food processor.

Divided the dough into 4 pieces. Roll out the dough to long finger size thick rolls, about 12-14 inches.

Line a cookie sheet with parchment paper and place the rolled dough onto the sheet.
Bake in the oven 325° F degrees for 12-18 minutes.

Cut the cookies when they are hot, into 1-inch sections. The cookies will harden when they have cooled.

Do not remove the cookies from the sheet, let them cool down completely, which takes about 17-20 minutes.

Chocolate Sections *Aka* Chocolate Brownie Cookie

7 oz margarine
7.7 oz granulate Sugar
9.7 oz all purpose flour
4-5 tbsp cocoa
1 tsp baking powder
1 tbsp vanilla sugar
1 egg

Topping:
1 egg
Pearl sugar

Yield: 40

Preheat the oven to 400° F degrees.

Attach the paddle attachment to the mixer. Place the butter in the mixing bowl, add the sugar.
Stir the butter and sugar well. Add one egg and stir again.
Mix the flour with the baking powder, vanilla sugar, and cocoa. Add the flour mix to the
butter mix.

Divide the dough into six equal pieces. Roll them out to 14-inch finger thick sticks, 3 on each
baking sheet.

Whisk one egg and brush each roll with the egg wash, sprinkle the pearl sugar on top of the
cookie.
Bake the cookies for 15-17 minutes in the middle of the oven. Take them out and cut the
cookies on the diagonal meanwhile they are hot.

Oatmeal Crisp

3.52 oz butter
¾ cup oatmeal
4.5 oz granulated sugar
2.5 oz Lyle's Golden Syrup
2 tbsp heavy whipping cream
2 oz all purpose flour
1 tsp baking powder
1 egg

Preheat the oven to 350° F degrees.

Melt the butter. Place the oatmeal in a large bowl. Pour the hot melted butter over oatmeal. Let it stand for 5 min.

Mix the all purpose flour with sugar, baking powder.
Pour the mixture over the oatmeal, add the golden syrup, cream, egg, and stir it all together into a batter.

Spoon out tsp size drops on a parchment paper lined baking sheet. 12 on one sheet, 4 x 3.

Bake in the oven for 8-9 minutes, let the cookies rest on the cookie sheet until they have cooled off, this takes about 10 minutes.

Toffee Crisp

Oven temperature:
Gas or Electric Oven: 400° F
Middle rack, 5 minutes

5.3 oz butter
6.3 oz granulated sugar
2.5 oz Lyle's Golden syrup
3.5 tbsp heavy whipping cream
3/4 cup oatmeal
3/4 cup unbleached flour
1/2 tsp baking powder
1 tsp vanilla sugar

Preheat the oven to 400° F.

Melt the butter in a pot with a thick bottom.

Add the rest of ALL the ingredients, and mix well.

Place a parchment paper on a baking sheet and place ½ tbsp size drops on the sheet, make only 8 drops per sheet, leave 2 inches of space between the drops.

Bake in the preheated oven for 5 minutes. Let them cool off completely before moving them to a plate.

Archipelago Cookie (hazelnut cookie)

Oven temperature:
Gas or Electric Oven: 350° F
Second lowest rack, 15 minutes

2 oz hazelnuts
5.3 oz butter
3 oz granulated sugar
6.3 oz unbleached flour
½ tsp baking powder

Attach the paddle attachment to the mixer. Place the butter in the mixing bowl, add the sugar, and stir butter and sugar creamy.

Chop the hazelnuts fine. Mix the nuts with the flour and baking powder.
Add that to the butter mix.

Dust the table with some flour.
Bring out the dough onto the flour, and kneed it together. When you have a nice firm shape, wrap it into plastic wrap, let the dough rest for 2 hours in the refrigerator.

Preheat the oven to 350° F.

Bring out the dough from the refrigerator; dust the table with some flour. Divide the dough in half, and use a rolling pin to roll out the dough to approximately 1/5 of an inch. Use a round cutter 2.5 inch in diameter.

Cut out 12 cookies and place them on a parchment paper lined cookie sheet.

Bake in the preheated oven for 15 minutes.

Chocolate Drop Cookies

2.11 oz powdered sugar
7 oz butter
2.82 oz potato starch flour
7.76 oz unbleached flour

3.52 oz dark chocolate chips

Preheat the oven to 350° F

Attach the paddle attachment to the mixer. Place the butter in the mixing bowl, mix sugar, and both flours, mix it together.

Divide the dough into 50 equal pieces. Roll them into small balls. Place the balls on a parchment paper lined baking sheet. Use the back of a wooden spoon, and make an indentation into middle of the ball, so it becomes a hole.

Bake the cookies for 10 minutes. Let them cool off completely.

Melt the chocolate in the microwave for 1 minute on high. If all the chocolate have not melted continue to stir, it will all melt together.

Checkerboard Cookies

8.11 oz unbleached all purpose flour
3 oz sugar
7 oz butter

Flavoring:
2 tbsp cocoa unsweetened
2 tsp vanilla sugar

Attach the paddle attachment to the mixer. Place the flour, sugar, butter into the mixing bowl. Mix the ingredients until it forms to firm dough.

Divide the dough into two equal parts. Mix one part with vanilla sugar, and one part with unsweetened cocoa.

Divide each part into two parts. Roll them out to equal lengths, all four parts.
Then place one part of each next to each other, do so with the other part of the dough as well, and place it onto the first set of dough, into a checkerboard pattern.
Push the dough's together slightly; wrap it up into plastic wrap and let it rest in the refrigerator for 1 hour.

Preheat the oven to 400° F degrees.

Take out the dough from the refrigerator and cut the dough into 1/5 of an inch thick.

Line a baking sheet with parchment paper, and place the cookies onto the sheet. Bake in the oven for 10 minutes.
Let them cool off before removing them.

Horseshoe Cookies

2 cups unbleached flour
6 oz granulated sugar
7 oz butter
1½ tbsp Lyle's Golden Syrup
½ tsp cardamom
2 tsp cinnamon
2 tsp baking soda

Oven temperature:
Gas or Electric Oven: 425° F
Second lowest rack, 7-8 minutes

Preheat the oven to 425° F degrees.

Attach the paddle attachment to the mixer. Place the flour, sugar, butter, syrup, cardamom, and cinnamon into the mixing bowl.

Dissolve the baking soda into 1 tbsp of water. Add that to the other ingredients that are already in the mixing bowl.

Mix it all together.

Divide the dough into 40 equal pieces; roll the out to thin length about 3 inches long. Bend them like a horseshoe. Place it on baking sheet that is lined with parchment paper.

Use a fork to push down on the cookies, all around the shape of the horseshoe.

You will fit about 9 cookies on one sheet.

Bake the cookies in the oven for 7-8 minutes. Let them cool off completely on the baking sheet before moving them.

Ginger Snaps

Full Batch:
6.6 oz water
3.4 oz light syrup or Lyle's Golden Syrup
2 tbsp ground cinnamon
1 tbsp ground cloves
1 tbsp ground ginger
1 tsp cardamom
1 tbsp baking soda
9.6 oz butter
2 cups sugar
2 lb flour

Yield 150

Half Batch:
3.3 oz water
1.7 oz light syrup or Lyle's Golden Syrup
1 tbsp ground cinnamon
½ tbsp ground cloves
½ tbsp ground ginger
½ tsp cardamom
½ tbsp baking soda
4.8 oz butter
1 cups sugar
1 lb flour

Yield 75

Day 1:
Let the water, syrup, spices, and baking soda come to a boil.
Mix butter and sugar in a large bowl, using the paddle attachment.
Pour the boiled spice mix over the butter and sugar mix, and let it cool down.
Now mix in almost all the flour (the rest will be used later).
Cover the dough in plastic or put it in a plastic zip lock bag. Let it rest until the next day.

Day 2:
Roll the dough thin, cut out the figures, and bake them for 5 minutes at 450° degree oven.

Melting Moments, an English Graham Cookie

10.6 oz butter
6.5 oz raw sugar
1 egg, lightly beaten
1 tsp vanilla sugar
6.9 oz graham flour
2 tsp baking powder
3.2 oz oatmeal
Extra oatmeal to roll the cookies in.

Preheat the oven to 350° F degrees.

Attach the paddle attachment to the mixer. Place the raw sugar and butter, into the mixing bowl, mix it creamy. Add the lightly beaten egg and vanilla sugar. Stir it in.

Mix the graham flour, oatmeal and baking powder in a separate bowl, and add the to the butter mix.

Divide the dough into 25 equal pieces, roll them into walnut size balls, and roll them into oatmeal.

Line a baking sheet with parchment paper, and place 6 balls on each sheet.

Bake them in the oven for 15-20 min. Let them cool off on the baking sheet.

King Karl XV's Pretzels

5.3 oz butter
4 tbsp heavy cream
7.8 oz unbleached all purpose flour

Garnish:
Water and Pearl Sugar

Preheat the oven to 400° F degrees.

Cream the butter, add the cream and the flour; mix it into working dough.

Divide the dough into 30 equal pieces.

Roll out each piece into 8 inches. Form them into pretzels. Line a baking sheet with parchment paper. Place the pretzel on the baking sheet, and brush them with water and sprinkle pearl sugar on top.

Bake them in the oven for 12 minutes.

Wiener sections

8.8 oz butter
4.6 oz granulated sugar
2 eggs
11.6 oz unbleached all purpose flour
½ tsp baking ammonia (baker's ammonia)

Filling:
Seedless Raspberry Jam not Preserve

Glaze:
¾ cup powdered sugar
1 ½ – 2 tbsp water

Preheat the oven to 400° F degrees.

Attach the paddle attachment to the mixer. Place the sugar and butter, into the mixing bowl, mix it.

Add the eggs one at the time, and stir after each egg until it is incorporated.
Mix the flour with the baking ammonia, add that to the butter mixture. Mix that until you have formed a smooth dough.

Divide the dough into 4; roll them out to 16 inches.
Line a baking sheet with parchment paper; place the 2 rolls on the baking sheet.

Make an indentation in middle of the roll, and place a string of jam in the indentation.
Bake in the middle of the oven for 15 minutes.

Meanwhile make the glaze, mix the sugar and water.

When they are done, take them out and let them sit for a minute, then drizzle the glaze right in the middle over the jam part.
Cut them on the diagonal while they are hot. You get about 15 cookies out of each roll, or 12 depending how thick you cut them.

Meringues

4 large egg whites
1/8 teaspoon cream of tartar
1/8 teaspoon salt
1 1/4 cups sugar
1 tablespoon cornstarch

Flavoring:

2 tbsp Vanilla Sugar

Or ½ cup Chopped nuts
Or 2 tablespoons of unsweetened cocoa (never flavor with liquid flavorings only dry products, such as spices, dried orange or lemon peel etc)

Yield: 70-80 meringues

Preheat convection oven to 200° F.

Mix 1/4 cup sugar, FLAVORING, and 1 tablespoon cornstarch in a separate bowl.

Place 4 egg whites, 1/8 teaspoon cream of tartar, and 1/8 teaspoon salt in the bowl of an electric mixer fitted with a balloon whip. Whisk on high speed until soft peeks form, about 1-2 minutes.

Gradually add 1 cup sugar while continuing to whisk on high speed. Whisk until stiff about 3 minutes.

Remove the bowl from the mixer and use a rubber spatula to fold in the sugar/cornstarch mix.

Fill a pastry bag (use tip of your choice (recommend no tip when using nuts as flavoring, just cut the piping bag) with meringue.

Pipe out the meringues on parchment paper covered sheets.

Bake the meringues for 2 hours and 15 minutes. Remove from the oven and allow the meringues to cool on baking sheet for 15 minutes before handling.

PS: Large meringues will acquire longer time in the oven.

NOTES

Pastries

Mazarin

Cookie Dough:
3.5 oz granulated sugar
7 oz butter
1 oz unbleached all purpose flour
1 egg
1/8 tsp baking ammonia
1/4 tsp vanilla sugar

Filling:
10 oz butter
1 lb almond paste
6 egg
1 ½ tsp vanilla sugar

Icing:
1 cup of powdered sugar
1 tbsp + 1 tsp water

Oven temperature:
Gas or Electric Oven: 350° F
Second Lowest rack, 25 minutes

Cream the butter with the sugar, add the egg. Mix the ammonia with the vanilla sugar and flour. Add the flour mix to the butter mix. Mix it well until incorporated. Let the dough rest over night in the refrigerator.

Preheat the oven to 350 degrees.

Mix 10.3 oz of almond paste with 6.5 oz of butter, and add 4 eggs, and 1 tsp vanilla sugar. Depending on the size of the food processor, this will let you make your filling in two batches. You can have this filling ready for a couple of days in the refrigerator. Do the same procedure with the remainder of the ingredients to the filling.

Place 25 fluted brioche tinned steel 2-3/4" diameter on a baking sheet. **(You can find these at www.bakedeco.com)** Roll out the dough to 1/5 inches thick. Stamp it out with a round shape cookie cutter 3.5 inches in diameter, and mold the dough piece into the round shaped brioche pastry molds.

Suggestion: You can put a 1 ½ tsp of jam in the bottom of each mold before you put the almond paste filling into the mold.

Fill the molds to the top with the filling. If you are using fruit filling put it first in the bottom and fill the rest of the cup with the almond paste filling mix. Bake the Mazarin's for 25 minutes

Make the icing, mix the sugar, and water. The icing should be thick and you should be able to spread with it. When the Mazarin's comes out of the oven let them cool off before spreading the icing on top. Let the icing dry before removing them from the molds.

Tosca Mazarin

Cookie Dough:
3.5 oz granulated sugar
7 oz butter
1 oz unbleached all purpose flour
1 egg
1/8 tsp baking ammonia
1/4 tsp vanilla sugar

Filling:
10 oz butter
1 lb almond paste
6 egg
1 ½ tsp vanilla sugar

Tosca Topping:
5.3 oz butter
1.5 oz granulated sugar
7.4 oz Lyle's golden syrup
3 tbsp unbleached all purpose flour
3 tbsp water
7 oz sliced almonds

Oven temperature:
Gas or Electric Oven: 350° F
Second Lowest rack, 25 minutes

Cream the butter with the sugar, add the egg. Mix the ammonia with the vanilla sugar and flour. Add the flour mix to the butter mix. Mix it well until incorporated. Let the dough rest over night in the refrigerator.

Preheat the oven to 350 degrees.

Mix 10.3 oz of almond paste with 6.5 oz of butter, and add 4 eggs, and 1 tsp vanilla sugar. Depending on the size of the food processor, this will let you make your filling in two batches. You can have this filling ready for a couple of days in the refrigerator. Do the same procedure with the remainder of the ingredients to the filling.

Place 25 fluted brioche tinned steel 2-3/4" diameter on a baking sheet. **(You can find these at www.bakedeco.com)** Roll out the dough to 1/5 inches thick. Stamp it out with a round shape cookie cutter 3.5 inches in diameter, and mold the dough piece into the round shaped brioche pastry molds.

Fill the molds to the top with the filling. Bake the Mazarin's for 18 minutes.

Meanwhile make the Tosca topping. Melt the butter in a pot; add sugar, Lyle's golden syrup, flour, and water. Let it all simmer together for 5 minutes. Add the sliced almonds to the mix.

Take out the Mazarin's, and spread the Tosca over them, put it back into the oven and let the Mazarin's finish baking for another 7 minutes, until the Tosca is bubbling, and have a nice amber color. Let them cool off before removing them from the molds.

Sarah Mazarin

Cookie Dough:
3.5 oz granulated sugar
7 oz butter
1 oz unbleached all purpose flour
1 egg
1/8 tsp baking ammonia
1/4 tsp vanilla sugar

Filling:
10 oz butter
1 lb almond paste
6 egg
1 ½ tsp vanilla sugar
1.7 oz Vanilla Jell-O™
2/3 cup milk (not fat free)
Applesauce or Apple Jam
2 tbsp granulated sugar
1 tsp cinnamon

Oven temperature:
Gas or Electric Oven: 350° F
Second Lowest rack, 20 minutes

Cream the butter with the sugar, add the egg. Mix the ammonia with the vanilla sugar and flour. Add the flour mix to the butter mix. Mix it well until incorporated. Let the dough rest over night in the refrigerator.

Preheat the oven to 350 degrees.

Mix 10.3 oz of almond paste with 6.5 oz of butter, and add 4 eggs, and 1 tsp vanilla sugar. Depending on the size of the food processor, this will let you make your filling in two batches. You can have this filling ready for a couple of days in the refrigerator. Do the same procedure with the remainder of the ingredients to the filling.

Mix the Jell-O with milk; this should be a little thick. Mix sugar and cinnamon.

Place 20 fluted brioche tinned steel 2-3/4" diameter on a baking sheet. (You can find these at www.bakedeco.com)

Roll out the dough to 1/5 inches thick. Stamp it out with a round shape cookie cutter 3.5 inches in diameter, and mold the dough piece into the round shaped brioche pastry molds.

Fill the molds 1/3 with applesauce or apple jam, 1/3 with almond paste filling, 1/3 with vanilla Jell-O crème. Take the cinnamon sugar mix and sprinkle that on top of all three fillings.

Roll out the dough to 1/5 inches thick. Stamp it out with a round shape cookie cutter 3 inches in diameter, and place the dough piece on top. Bake the Mazarin's for 20 minutes. Let them cool off before removing them from the molds.

Dust the top with powdered sugar before serving.

Helena Pastry

Cookie Dough:

8 oz unbleached all purpose flour
4.4 oz butter
2 tbsp ice cold water

Filling:
3.5 oz almonds
1 ¼ cup powdered sugar
3 small egg whites or 2 large egg whites

Oven temperature:
Gas or Electric Oven: 350° F
Second Lowest rack, 20 minutes

Place the flour in a food processor, and cut the butter into pieces, push the pulse button 10 times on the food processor, add the water, and let the food processor quickly pull together the dough. Wrap the dough in plastic wrap and let it rest for a couple of hours in the refrigerator.

In the mean time, blanch the almonds and peel them. Use the food processor and grind them up, add the powdered sugar, and mix it together, add last the egg whites.

Take out the dough from the refrigerator. Dust the table with some flour, and roll out part of the dough. Roll out the dough to 1/8 inches thick. Place 15 fluted brioche tinned steel 2-3/4" diameter on a baking sheet. **(You can find these at www.bakedeco.com)**

Stamp it out with a round shape cookie cutter 3.5 inches in diameter, and mold the dough piece into the round shaped brioche pastry molds.

Fill the molds to the top with the filling. Roll out the rest of the dough to 1/5 inches thick. Use a serrated cutter and make long strips, ¼ inch wide. Place the strips in a cross wise pattern on each mold.

Bake in the oven for 20 minutes. When you pull them out of the oven, let them cool off before unmolding them.

Lemon Linz

8 oz unbleached all purpose flour
2.8 oz potato starch flour
3 oz granulated sugar
7 oz butter

Filling:
Your choice of lemon curd or other lemon filling
available at the store

Mix all the ingredient to the dough, let it rest for a couple of hours.

Place 12 fluted brioche tinned steel 2-3/4" diameter on a baking sheet. **(You can find these at www.bakedeco.com)** Roll out the dough to 1/5 inches thick. Stamp it out with a round shape cookie cutter 3.5 inches in diameter, and mold the dough piece into the round shaped brioche pastry molds

Fill the mold with the lemon filling.
Roll out the dough to 1/5 inches thick. Stamp it out with a round shape cookie cutter 3 inches in diameter, and place the dough piece on top. Bake the pastry for 15 minutes. Let them cool off before removing them from the molds.

Dust the top with powdered sugar before serving.

Maria Cream Puffs

Oven temperature:
Gas or Electric Oven: 350° F
Second Lowest rack, 45 minutes

Cookie dough on top:
120 gr. unbleached flour
3 tbsp sugar
75 gr. butter

Petit-Choux Dough:
300 ml water
100 gr. butter
120 gr. unbleached all purpose flour
3 medium eggs

Filling
1.5 cups heavy whipping cream
4 oz raspberry filling
8 oz Bavarian cream (Make one batch of the pastry cream on page 86. Take 1 ¼ cup pastry cream from the batch. Fold in ½ cup of whipped heavy cream into the pastry cream. **Do the pastry cream one day a head.**)

Garnish:
Powdered Sugar

Make first the cookie dough by mixing all the ingredients to dough. Let it rest a little in the refrigerator.

Roll out the dough 1/5 inch thick on the counter, and stamp out ten 2 inch rounds. Place the dough pieces on a parchment paper and put it back into the refrigerator for later use.

Preheat the oven to 350°F. Dress a sheet pan with parchment paper.

Put the water and butter in a saucepan and bring to the boil. Add the flour and stir until the mixture no longer sticks to the sides of the pan. Take the saucepan off the heat.

Put the knife attachment into the food processor.
Place dough into the food processor; let it cool off a minute or two. Attach the top of the food processor and add then one egg at the time while it is moving on the highest speed. When all the eggs are incorporated well fill the dough into a piping bag.

Pipe out 10 equal size rounds, take out the cookie dough pieces from the refrigerator, place one piece of cookie dough on each piped out petit-choux round.

Place the sheet pan immediately into the oven and bake the pastries for 45 minutes. DO NOT OPEN THE OVEN DOOR OR THEY WILL BE RUINED.

Filling the pastries:

When the pastries are done, let them cool off completely.

Prepare the fillings. Whip the cream, and place it into a piping bag, store it in the refrigerator, fill another piping bag with raspberry filling or seedless raspberry jam.
Last, make the Bavarian cream, also fill the Bavarian cream in to a piping bag.

When the pastries are cooled off, take a small peering knife, and cut a small hole underneath the petit-choux pastry. Cut off the end of the piping bags, not too big.

Fill first with the whipped cream, then take the raspberry piping bag and fill some of that into the pastry, finally pipe some of the Bavarian cream until it is filled but not so that the pastry will pop. This will be a trial and error the first one you make, but you will get the hang of it.

Repeat the same procedure with the rest. Place the pastries on large paper cups. Finish off with sifting powdered sugar on top of each.

Cakes

Tortes

Chocolate Dream Cake

Meringue:
4 egg whites
1/8 teaspoon cream of tartar
1/8 teaspoon salt
1 1/4 cups sugar
2 tablespoons unsweetened cocoa, sifted
1-tablespoon cornstarch

Preheat oven to 225° F.

Using an 8-inch cake circle as a guide, with a pencil trace a circle on a sheet parchment paper. Turn the paper over and with trace mark down, place on a baking sheet.

Mix 1/4 cup sugar, cocoa, and 1 tablespoon cornstarch in a separate bowl.

Place 4 egg whites, 1/8 teaspoon cream of tartar, and 1/8 teaspoon salt in the bowl of an electric mixer fitted with a balloon whip. Whisk on high speed until soft peeks form, about 1-2 minutes.

Gradually add 1 cup sugar while continuing to whisk on high speed. Whisk until stiff about 3 minutes. Remove the bowl from the mixer and use a rubber spatula to fold in sugar/cornstarch mix.

Fill a pastry bag (with no tip) with cocoa meringue. Fill the traced circle with meringue: start in the center and pipe a 3/4-inch wide spiral towards the outside of the circle. With the rest of the meringue, drop out 8-10 meringue kisses, this is for garnish later.

Place the meringue in the preheated oven and bake for 15 minutes. Reduce heat to 200 degrees F. and bake for 2 hours and 45 minutes. Remove from the oven and allow the cocoa meringue to cool on baking sheet for 45 minutes before handling.

Adjust the oven temperature to 425 degrees F.

Make the Cake, see recipe for "French Chocolate Cake pg. 81" Make it an 8-inch cake.

Chocolate Mousse:
3 oz semisweet chocolate, broken into ½ oz pieces
¾ Cup heavy cream
1 egg white
1 tablespoons sugar

  While the meringue is baking, prepare the chocolate mousse. Heat 1-inch of water in the bottom half of a double boiler over medium heat. Place 3-ounces of semisweet chocolate in the top half of the double boiler. Tightly cover the top with film wrap. Allow the chocolate to melt slowly, about 9 to 10 minutes. Remove from the heat and stir until smooth keep at room temperature until needed.

  Place 1 1/2 cups heavy whipping cream in the well-chilled bowl of an electric mixer fitted with a well-chilled balloon whip. Whisk on high speed until peaks form, about 1 minute. Set aside for a few minutes until needed.

  Whisk 1 egg white in a large stainless-steel bowl, until soft peaks form, about 3 minutes. Add 1 tablespoons sugar and continue to whisk until stiff peaks form, about 2 to 2 1/2 minutes. Add a 1/4 of the whipped cream to the chocolate and whisk quickly, vigorously, and thoroughly, then add to the egg whites. Now add the remaining whipped cream. Fold all together gently but thoroughly. Refrigerate the chocolate mousse until needed.

Chocolate Ganache:
For filling:
1/2 cup heavy cream
1 tablespoon unsalted butter
7.3 oz semisweet chocolate, broken into ½-ounce pieces

  Prepare the ganache; heat ¾-cup heavy cream and 1 ½ tablespoons of butter in a 2 1/2 quart saucepan over medium high heat. Bring to a boil. Place 11 ounces of semisweet chocolate in a stainless-steel bowl. Pour the boiling cream over the chocolate and allow to stand for 5 minutes. Stir until smooth. Keep at room temperature until needed.

Chocolate Glaze:
½ cup heavy cream
1 ½ tablespoon unsalted butter
11 oz semisweet chocolate, broken into ½-ounce pieces

Make the chocolate glaze the same way you made the chocolate ganache filling.

To assemble Death by Chocolate:

Place a closed 8x3 inch spring form pan on a baking sheet. Set the top half of the chocolate cake inside the pan, top side up. Ladle 1 1/2 cups of ganache into the pan over the chocolate cake.

Trim the cocoa meringue with a serrated knife so that it will fit tightly into the pan. Place the trimmed cocoa meringue, top side up, inside the pan on top of the ganache, pressing down gently on the cocoa meringue to eliminate air pockets.

Spoon the mocha mousse on top of the cocoa meringue, spreading evenly. Place the remaining chocolate cake half-bottom side up, on top of the mocha mousse. Chill the cake in the freezer for 30 minutes or refrigerate for 1 hour. Remove the cake from the freezer and cut around the edges to release from the spring form pan.

Pour the remaining ganache over the cake and use a cake spatula to spread the ganache evenly over the top of sides of the cake. Refrigerate the cake for Death by Chocolate for at least 4 hours, and preferably 12 hours, before cutting and serving.

To serve, cut the Death by Chocolate into the desired number of servings. Heat the blade of a serrated knife under hot running water before slicing into the cake. Really, it is more about melting through the cake than cutting it Repeat this procedure after cutting each slice.

Princess Torte

1 genoise yellow cake pg. 50
1 ¼ cup pastry cream pg. 98
¾ cup of red raspberry filling or seedless jam
1 ½ cup of heavy whipping cream
2 tsp vanilla sugar
11 oz of Odense marzipan
green food coloring
powdered sugar

1. Make one 8-inch round Genoise cake on page 50. Cut the cake into two layers.

   Whip the heavy cream firm, and fold in 2 tsp of vanilla sugar.

   Make one batch of the pastry cream on page 98. Take 1 ¼ cup pastry cream from the batch. Fold in ½ cup of whipped heavy cream into the pastry cream.

2. Spread the raspberry filling or jam on the bottom layer, place another cake layer on top, and spread the pastry cream on the second layer. Place the top on, and place all the heavy whipped cream on top of the cake. Spread some of the cream around it, but most of it on top in a dome shape style. Place the cake in the refrigerator.

3. Color the Odense Marzipan, with 1 drop of the food coloring. Be careful to not use too much color.

4. Dust the counter with powdered sugar, and roll out the marzipan about 1/5 inches thick.

5. Dust powdered sugar on occasion so the marzipan does not stick on the counter, but not too much, this you have to be careful with.

6. Roll up the round shaped rolled out marzipan on a narrow rolling pin. Bring out the cake from the refrigerator, and roll off the marzipan starting from one side to the other. Lightly dress the cake with the marzipan, smooth out any creases, and cut off excess of marzipan at the very bottom.

7. Sift powdered sugar over the cake. Place the cake back in the refrigerator until ready to eat. .This cake should not be sitting out in room temperature due to the components in the cake, such as cream, and pastry cream.

Budapest Roll

¾ cup + 1 tbsp or approx 6 egg whites
1 1/3 cup granulated sugar
6 tbsp Vanilla Jell-O Pudding Powder
3.5 oz finely ground Hazelnuts

Filling
1 1/3 cup heavy whipping cream
4 peach halves cut into smaller pieces, or maraschino cherries
1 tbsp of vanilla sugar

Decoration
Melted Chocolate to drizzle on top,
Or Powdered Sugar to dust on top,
Or Cocoa Powder to dust on top

Turn on the oven to 350 degrees F.

Whisk the egg whites until you get thick and large firm peaks this will take about 5-7 minutes.
Slow down the beaters and in a steady pace whisk in the sugar.
Speed up the beaters and beat for 3-4 minutes until the sugar is completely incorporated.

Meanwhile, mix the nuts with the Jell-O pudding powder.
Fold in the nut mixture with a balloon whisk.
Fill a piping bag with the meringue.

Dress a baking sheet with parchment paper, pipe out the meringue in long strips, until you have covered the entire sheet. Bake the meringue for 20 minutes.

When you take out the meringue, place a another piece of parchment paper on top of the baked meringue, and place another baking sheet on top of the parchment paper, then flip the pan's over.

Remove the pan that is on top now, and peel off the parchment paper that the meringue is baked on. Do it quick and careful, pull in a steady pace. Let the meringue cool off completely.

Whip the cream, add the vanilla sugar. Spread the cream on top of the meringue, scatter the peach pieces on top, and roll it up from along its width.

French Chocolate Cake

5 oz semi-sweet chocolate
1.2 oz butter
3 eggs (separate the egg yolks from the whites)
6 ½ tbsp granulated sugar
6 ½ tbsp all purpose flour
1 tsp baking powder
1 tbsp hazelnut liqueur or rum

Glaze:
2.3 oz butter
4 oz milk chocolate chips
1 oz semi-sweet chocolate
1 tsp hazelnut liqueur or rum

Servings: 16

Preheat the oven to 425° F degrees.

   Break the semi-sweet chocolate into a bowl and add the 1.2 oz of butter, melt stirring in a Bain Marie. (Bain-Marie= (Mary's bath) refers to the method of placing a pan of food in another pan with water in it to stabilize the heat reaching the food (water bath).
Put the egg yolks in a large bowl. Beat them with the sugar until the mixture falls in a ribbon.
   Then add the flour mixed with the baking powder, the chocolate butter mixture, and the Hazelnut liqueur. Mix well.

   Whisk the egg whites with a pinch of salt to stiff peaks and fold the carefully into the batter. Generously grease an 8' inch round cake pan with some butter, put a piece of parchment paper fitting only the bottom of the pan, and pour the batter into the pan.
   Bake for 10 minutes in 425° F, then reduce the heat to 350° F and bake additional 8 minutes. Remove the cake from the oven and leave it to cool.

For the Glaze:
   Put the 2.3 oz butter, 4 oz milk chocolate chips, 1 oz semi-sweet chocolate, and the 2 tbsp of Hazelnut liqueur into a bowl, and melt it in a Bain Marie. Stir, melt it all together. Pour the melted mixture evenly over the cake and let it run down over the edges
   Leave it until completely cool before serving

Tiramisu

6 egg yolks
3 tablespoons sugar
1 pound mascarpone cheese
1 1/2 cups strong espresso, cooled
¼ cup Port wine
24 packaged ladyfingers
1/4 cup dark chocolate shavings, for garnish

In a large bowl, using an electric mixer with whisk attachment, beat egg yolks and sugar until thick and pale, about 5 minutes. Add mascarpone cheese and beat until smooth. Add 1 tablespoon of espresso and mix until thoroughly combined.

In a small shallow dish, add remaining espresso and port wine. Dip each ladyfinger into espresso for only 5 seconds. Letting the ladyfingers soak too long will cause them to fall apart. Place the soaked ladyfinger on the bottom of a 13 by 9 inch baking dish, breaking them in half if necessary in order to fit the bottom.

Spread evenly 1/2 of the mascarpone mixture over the ladyfingers. Shave chocolate over the mascarpone layer, repeat this procedure until all the ladyfingers and mascarpone mixture is gone, and top off with a lot of shaved chocolate..

Cover tiramisu with plastic wrap and refrigerate for at least 2 hours, up to 8 hours.

Before serving, sprinkle with chocolate shavings.

Crisp Cake w/ Vanilla Crème
Oven Temperature 257° F Degrees

Meringue Bottom:
4 egg whites
6.7 oz granulated sugar
10 oz Rice Crispies®
Vanilla Crème:
4 egg yolks
3.4 oz sugar
3.4 oz heavy whipping cream
3.0 oz butter in small cubes
1 tbsp vanilla sugar
Topping:
1 ½ cup heavy whipping cream, whipped
3 cups fresh berries, e.g. strawberries, raspberries, blueberries, etc.

Servings: 8-10

Turn on the oven to 257° F degrees.
Separate the egg white and yolks. Put the yolks aside for the butter cream.

Place the egg whites in a clean bowl and start whisking them until you have soft peaks.

Add the sugar, 2 oz at a time until it all has been incorporated. Fold in the Rice Crispies®.
Line a baking sheet with parchment paper, and butter it. (Normally you do not need to butter a parchment paper; however, this momentum is very important in his recipe.)

Spread out the meringue on the parchment paper evenly and into 14 x 11 inch rectangle.
Bake the meringue in the oven for 65 minutes at 257° F degrees.

Meanwhile the meringue is baking make the crème :
Mix egg yolks, sugar, whipping cream, in a saucepan, simmer it until it has thickened. Be very careful so the egg yolk does not curdle.
Take the sauce off the heat, continue to whisk it in cold water bath until the cream is lukewarm, now add the butter cubes, a little at time until all of the butter is incorporated and completely smooth. Finally incorporate the vanilla sugar. Put the butter cream in the refrigerator to stiff up a little.

Assembling the cake:
Divide the meringue sheet in half, spread the butter cream onto on side of the meringue sheet, put the other meringue half on top.
Whip up some whipping cream and spread it over the top. Garnish generously with fresh fruit of your choice.

Chocolate Toffee Pie w/ Blueberries

3.5 oz butter
1.5 oz granulated sugar
4.2 oz oatmeal
3 oz unbleached all purpose flour

Filling:
2/3 cup heavy whipping cream
1.75 oz butter
2/3 cup Lyle's Golden Syrup
7 oz semi sweet dark chocolate
2/3 cup blueberries

Serve with heavy whipped cream

Preheat the oven to 400 °F degrees.

Melt the butter in a saucepan. Add the sugar, oatmeal, and flour. Stir it together into a dough. Press out the dough in to a pie crust 9 inches diameter.

Pre cook the crust in the middle of the oven for 8-10 minutes, until it has received a nice color.

Place cream, butter, and syrup in saucepan, and bring it to a boil; simmer on low heat for 10 minutes, turn off the stove.

Chop the chocolate into smaller pieces, and put it into the saucepan. Place it back on the heat, but do not turn on the heat. Stir the chocolate until it has melted and is smooth and shiny. Pour the chocolate mixture into the pie crust, drizzle the blueberries on top.

Place it into the refrigerator to cool off and set up, 5 hours or over night.

Serve the pie with lightly whipped cream.

Sandwich Cakes

Skagen Cake

Skagen Filling:

One 9-inches round white bread, page 24.

3 eggs, hardboiled, and chopped fine
12 oz Precooked Shrimp
12 oz Snow crab
1/3 cup mayonnaise
1/3 cup crème fraiche
¼ tsp salt
¼ tsp pepper, preferably white pepper
¼ cup of freshly chopped dill
1 tablespoon of freshly squeezed lemon juice

Garnishing Crème
4 oz Philadelphia cheese (if you don't have a food processor, make sure you let the cheese sit out for an hour)
2 oz crème fraiche
3 oz Alouette™ Cheese (parmesan & peppercorn, there is many more flavors, use what you feel is right for you)

Garnishing:
6 oz Smoked Salmon
(fold each slice horizontally, and roll it up from one side, this will be a rose when it is turned over. It also depends how large the slices are. If they are narrower slices, just roll it up and stand them up, it will be the same effect)
3 oz Large precooked shrimp w/ shell (before garnishing, remove the shells)
Red or Black Caviar or Row (optional)
1 lemon / slices
1 European hot house cucumber/ slices
Dill
Butter Lettuce / rinsed and patted dry

Instructions:

Let the shrimp and the snow crab drain from all its water. Place them between your hands and squeeze lightly to get most of the water out of them.

Place all the remainder of the ingredients for the filling into a bowl, and mix them up, add the shrimp and snow crab and toss it together.

Cut the bread loaf horizontally into three layers.

Put half of the spread on the bottom piece, place another layer on top, and lay the rest of the filling on that layer, place the top lid on top.

In your food processor, place the Philadelphia cheese, crème fraiche, and the Alouette cheese, and mix it all up until smooth. (If you don't have a food processor, use a fork, however, make sure the cheeses are soft.) Spread the mixture evenly around the entire cake. Place the leaves of butter lettuce around the cake.

Garnish the top with roses made out of the salmon in a round circle; place the precooked shrimp in the middle as you please. Place slices of cucumber, lemon, in-between the salmons and top of with dill on each salmon rose, add some red or black caviar in the middle on top of the shrimp.

The cake should stay in the refrigerator until serving.

Vegetarian Cake

One 9-inches round white bread, page 24

7 oz Greek feta cheese
8 oz Quark, regular
1/3 cup Ajvar Relish

Garnering:
4 oz Philadelphia cheese (if you don't have a food processor, make sure you let the cheese sit out for an hour)
2 oz crème fraiche
3 oz Alouette™ Cheese (parmesan & peppercorn, there is many more flavors, use what you feel is right for you)
Arugula lettuce
Cherry Tomatoes, yellow and red, cut in half,
½ tsp salt
1 pinch black pepper

Idea: You can toss the cherry tomatoes in balsamic vinaigrette and place them on top of the arugula lettuce.

Mix the feta, quark, and Ajvar Relish together into a smooth filling.

Cut the bread loaf horizontally into three layers.

Put half of the spread on the bottom piece, place another layer on top, and lay the rest of the filling on that layer, place the top lid on top.

In your food processor, place the Philadelphia cheese, crème fraiche, and the Alouette cheese, and mix it all up until smooth. (If you don't have a food processor, use a fork, however, make sure the cheeses are soft.) Spread the mixture evenly around the entire cake. Place the arugula lettuce around the cake.
Place the cherry tomatoes on top and season with salt and black pepper, or you can toss the cherry tomatoes in balsamic vinaigrette and then place them on top of the arugula lettuce.

The cake should stay in the refrigerator until serving.

Traditional Sandwich Cake
(Lunch Meat Version)

One 9-inches round white bread, page 24.

<u>Pate filling:</u>
1 package Liver pate
¼ cup sweet cucumber pickles
1 small jar of crushed pineapples
1/3 cup heavy whipping cream
¼ cup chopped parsley

Or

Ham filling:
16 slices of smoked ham, chopped
4 inch of leek, mostly the white part, finely chopped
¼ cup red onion, finely chopped
3 slices of pineapple from a can, chopped fine
¾ cup crème fraiche
4 tbsp mayonnaises

<u>Garnishing Crème:</u>
4 oz Philadelphia cheese (if you don't have a food processor, make sure you let the cheese sit out for an hour)
2 oz crème fraiche
3 oz Alouette Cheese (parmesan & peppercorn, there is many more flavors, use what you feel is right for you)

<u>Garnishing for the top:</u>
10 toothpicks
10 slices of Smoked ham, rolled up like trumpets
10 slices of Turkey, smoked, honey, peppercorn any kind you like, rolled them up like trumpets
10 slices of Cheese, Swiss or Gouda, roll them up like logs
10 cherry tomatoes
European hot house cucumber/ slices
10 black olives or green olives, depends on what you like
Mandarin Oranges (fruit is very refreshing on a sandwich cake, and it really works)
Butter Lettuce / rinsed and patted dry

<u>FYI: You can add shrimp to a sandwich cake that has turkey and ham on it.</u>

<u>Pate Filling:</u>
Place all the ingredients for the filling into a bowl, and mix them up, or use your food processor to mix them smooth.

<u>Ham filling:</u>
Mix all the ingredients by hand. Do not use food processor.

Cut the bread loaf horizontally into three layers. Put half of the spread on the bottom piece, place another layer on top, and lay the rest of the filling on that layer, place the top lid on top.

In your food processor, place the Philadelphia cheese, crème fraiche, and the Alouette cheese, and mix it all up until smooth. (If you don't have a food processor, use a fork, however, make sure the cheeses are soft.) Spread the mixture evenly around the entire cake. Place the leaves of butter lettuce around the cake. Garnish the top with the turkey and ham, in a round circle on top.

Take the toothpick and thread the cherry tomato first, then add the rolled up cheese slice. Stick the toothpick around the cake with even space. Continue to garnish with slices of cucumbers, and black olives or green in the middle.

The cake should stay in the refrigerator until serving.

Miscellaneous

Almond Paste

10.6 oz   almonds
9.5 oz   powdered sugar
1/3 cup   egg whites or pasteurized egg whites
1 tsp   almond extract

Blanch the almonds, and peel them.
 Grind almonds in a food processor, add
the powdered sugar, grind the nuts, and
sugar together for one minute.
 Add the egg whites or the pasteurized egg
whites + 1 tsp almond extract

Pastry Cream

1 cup whole milk
1/3 cup sugar
2 tbsp cornstarch
3 large egg yolks
2 tbsp unsalted butter
2 tsp vanilla sugar

Combine ¾ cup of milk and the sugar in a
small saucepan, and place over low heat.

In a bowl, add ¼ cup of milk, cornstarch,
and egg yolks, whisk it together.
 When the milk boils, whisk 1/3 of it into
the milk/egg/cornstarch mix.

 Place the saucepan back on to the heat
and bring it back up to boil, whisk the milk,
while whisking pour the
milk/cornstarch/egg/milk mixture into the
saucepan and whisk until it thickens and
comes to a full boil, about 15 seconds.
 Take it off the heat immediately, and
continue to whisk, add the butter and
vanilla sugar, and whisk it in.
 Pour the pastry cream into a glass bowl,
and wrap plastic wrap over it, press down
the plastic wrap over the surface of the
pastry cream so "no skin" will be created
while resting in the refrigerator for 24
hours.

Lemon Crème

1 ¼ cup heavy cream
1/3 cup lemon juice
1 tbsp corn starch
5 egg yolks
2/3 cup sugar

Scold the cream in a heavy bottomed stainless steel pot.
Meanwhile stir together, lemon juice, corn starch, egg yolks, and sugar in a bowl.

Temper the egg yolks by adding a little hot cream at the time, and stir vigorously. After all the cream has been added into the bowl, return it all into the pot, and simmer on low heat.

Whisk constantly so the crème doesn't turn to scramble eggs. Remove the pot from the heat after the crème has thickened, and place the pot in an ice-water bath. Continue to whisk until the crème has cooled off.

Place the crème in a clean glass bowl, cover with plastic wrap, and press it down over the surface, and put it in the refrigerator for 8-24 hours.

Ideas:

Pastry for Easter:
Make your traditional jelly roll pg. 52, cut into thick pieces, place the piece with the cut side up, in a large white paper cup.
Drain a can of apricots or half peaches. Dry them a little, and place it in the middle of the jelly roll. Whip heavy whipping cream, and pipe the cream around the yellow fruit. A pastry the looks like an 'egg', and yet sweet and not savory.

Princess Pastry:
The marzipan can be colored in different colors, make a bow of marzipan for decoration, instead of using the pastry cream, use the lemon crème, fresh fruit such as raspberries will work great instead of raspberry filling. Whip the cream and top it off with a top of marzipan.

Meringues:
Instead of making small meringues, pipe out birds nest, fill them with lemon crème and fresh berries and whipped cream.

Sundried Tomato & Black Olive Bread:
If you like Panini's, this bread makes your Panini taste like an expensive high end restaurant sandwich, you will never go out for another sandwich again.

Sandwich Cakes:
You can use mascarpone cheese mixed with sundried tomatoes, and layer with Italian meats in between on top of the mascarpone mix, garnish with more meats, cheeses, black olives, tomatoes.

Scones:
The scone recipe in this book is excellent to make a head and freeze, and can be taken out of the freezer frozen and baked immediately in 350 °F degrees for 18-20 minutes, all depending on size.

Cardamom Braids:
Make them and bake them, and freeze them while they are little warm. The bag will create moisture, which will fall back into the bread, which will retain its moisture, and when you take them out the will have fresh baked taste.

Instead of Braids:
Instead of cutting them into braids, cut them into 2 inches thick slices, and place them up with the cut side into a disposable baking pan, place 7 buns together. Let them rise accordingly, brush egg wash on them and sprinkle pearl sugar and sliced almond on top, bake in preheated 425°F oven, for 20-25 minutes.

WHERE TO BUY

Companies that provides special ingredients, equipment, packaging etc...

www.bakedeco.com
Products, special Ingredients, baking molds and equipment

www.fantes.com
Kitchenware shop, baking essentials, molds, baking

www.boisecoop.com
Special ingredients, baking products

www.lorannoils.com
Special ingredients, flavorings

www.novacartusa.com
This site is directed to those who own a business only.

www.plasticcontainercity.com
This site provides containers for baking to retail customers.

www.spicesetc.com
Spices, rubs, sauce etc.

Index, Alphabetic

www.ingramcontent.com/pod-product-compliance
Lightning Source LLC
Chambersburg PA
CBHW081235090426
42738CB00016B/3318